Aphorisms

Aphorisms

Brief Bursts of Truth

DONALD PATRICK REDHEFFER

APHORISMS
BRIEF BURSTS OF TRUTH

iUniverse books may be ordered through booksellers or by contacting:

iUniverse
1663 Liberty Drive
Bloomington, IN 47403
www.iuniverse.com
1-800-Authors (1-800-288-4677)

ISBN: 978-1-5320-0144-4 (sc)
ISBN: 978-1-5320-0145-1 (hc)
ISBN: 978-1-5320-0143-7 (e)

Library of Congress Control Number: 2016910602

Print information available on the last page.

iUniverse rev. date: 08/11/2016

To Joselita

Wealth is not found in rings and things
in mansions on the shore;
you are the greatest joy life brings,
the one whom I adore.

In Memoriam

Robert Joseph Smythe never failed to be my friend.

Contents

Also by Donald Patrick Redheffer

Musings of a Meandering Stream (2008)

Streams of Thought (2009)

Reply to Oblivion (2010)

Sense and Sound (2012)

Acknowledgments

My sincere gratitude to Robert Smythe, Ronald Kaufman, Gwyneth Arounvong, Pray Arounvong, Marjorie Mendoza, Jason Laroco, Judy Redheffer, and Mark Castiglia, who have encouraged the writing of this book. Special thanks to my wife, Joselita, for typing the text.

Aphorisms

Brief bursts of truth
are what remain
of writing made to last.

There is no patience
with long trains
of boorish bombast.

Preface

It is my hope that these aphorisms will enrich
the old and bring something of the new.

An aphorism is a brief expression of a truth or sentiment.
Although truth cares nothing for how we feel, sentiment
is replete with values and emotion. In either case,
the aphorism truly expresses a point of view.

The penchant of the aphorist to challenge cherished
belief will inevitably offend some readers.

This writer's goal is to provoke thought, not inspire belief.

Prologue

My writings come from a place
enriched by heart and mind,
where one stares into empty space
for hours at a time,
pursuing the sublime.

Ability

1. Even great ability requires at least a tincture of praise to bring it to fruition.

2. Greatness can be the chief obstacle to popularity.

3. Those who encourage us to develop and use our abilities overlook the gifted criminals among us who do unspeakable harm.

4. Those without ability enshrine mediocrity.

Absence

5. Absence augments whatever you once thought or felt.

6. Love makes life exponential, whereas absence is loss without end.

7. The absence felt at one's side is not far from death.

8. There is an absence I can see
   that leaves no thing sublime;
   to truly love is ecstasy
   found only once in time.

9. To Joselita: life without you is empty breath.

Absolutes

10.   Hatred can be beautiful, and love can be ugly; so much for absolutes.

Abstinence

11.   Our vices succumb to abstinence alone, for moderation tempts with every taste.

12.   Repeated abstinence vanishes into an equilibrium where there is no feeling of denial.

Abstractions

13.   Abstractions fly far above the experience that gave them birth. They find meaning in the familiar.

14.   Abstractions slowly arise from the bloody encounters of experience, hoping to give meaning to what at the time seemed no more than the struggle to endure.

15.   Abstractions store the most meaning in the least space.

16.   Algebra is an abstraction of arithmetic.

17.   Subtraction is the key
to abstraction's allure.
Take away more and more
till you're left with the pure.

18. There are brilliant abstractions found in the rarefied air of mathematics and philosophy. Most of us need examples to bring these truths back down to earth.

Absurdity

19. Absurdity is found everywhere when we contemplate the cosmic disaster that confronts our race.

20. Our needs create absurdities that are at times life sustaining.

21. We embrace absurdity when it suits our fancy.

Abuse

22. Abuse of what is bad should go by another name.

23. Only the worthy merit abuse.

24. Those without merit are rarely abused.

Acceptance

25. Acceptance is the hallmark of the follower, allowing what *is* to define morality.

26. Acceptance of a gift, some say,
is full of strings that tie;
those found too quickly to repay
simply verify
what words cannot deny.

27. To accept all is to commit to an amoral and
thoughtless existence.

28. To be accepted by multitudes, it is best to leave
the most important questions unanswered.

Accident

29. Accidents only appear to escape the natural law to
which we are all subject.

30. The notion of an accident requires a degree of
disorder some find uncomfortable.

Accomplishment

31. To do what we see as great,
spend every day denying fate
its final move—our checkmate.

Accusation

32. Accusations mark us for life.

Achievement

33.　Achievement reveals the immensity of what is yet to be done.

34.　Chance weaves its way into every aspect of life, putting achievement in proper perspective.

35.　Does our awareness of the universe imbue us with significance beyond our fragile presence on this planet?

36.　Great achievement is found to be possible by challenging the improbable.

37.　There is consistency in mediocrity not seen in the peaks and valleys of greatness.

38.　Those focused on forefathers are admitting they have nothing significant to contribute.

39.　What appears to be done easily is often the result of diligent preparations.

Acquaintance

40.　Heirs who divide a great fortune are more than acquaintances.

Acting

41. Actors vanish into the characters they portray, hoping never to reappear.

42. The honest hypocrisy of acting has inspired the devotion of millions—so much for genuine good works.

43. There is no skill more important for surviving encounters with humanity than acting.

44. We are all actors, most of us off the stage.

Action

45. An action can arise from many points of view and should be measured by its impact, not its reason.

46. Every act is a decision to not do something else. From the trivial to the profound, our actions define us.

47. Every action is a reaction against something.

48. Good deeds surpass fine feelings.

49. Implementing ideals can result in a Nazi Germany.

50. The peace that comes from actively pursuing and accomplishing some goal can be amoral.

51.   Those who favor action over words have ignored the carnage that comes from men of action.

52.   To leave nothing to chance is to never act.

53.   When we give time and money to victims of catastrophe, our motives are of little relevance.

Adam and Eve

54.   The first man slept in guiltless bliss,
until from Adam's rib Eve came;
alone no more, his spirit soared
for love had come to claim
his soul now bound for shame.

Adaptability

55.   Adapt or perish is the rule,
for nature's winds are strong;
give and take and do not mistake
the right path for the wrong.

Addiction

56.   There are addictions that make apathy seem sublime.

Administration

57. The administration is a creation of expediency where the impulse to seek profound truth or artistic beauty is rarely found.

Admiration

58. Admiration for some special ability is understandable, but when extended to the entire human being, it is more than misguided.

59. Admiration ignores the details.

60. Admiration should not be confused with love. We may despise those we admire.

61. The more we know, the less we admire.

62. The stage inspires admiration rarely given a sage.

63. Being admired by some is an insult.

64. We are reluctant to admire those who were not born with some special gift.

Adoration

65. Adoration blindly sees what it wishes to see.

66. Adoration sees beyond the many flaws to the beauty within; it is the ultimate joy.

Adult

67. The distinction between adult and child is more arbitrary than real. At each stage, we are confronted by difficulties that can bring us down. We all need help every step of the way.

Advancement

68. The higher you go, the lower you reach.

Advantage

69. Taking advantage can be more predatory than humane. We are defined by what we are willing to do to succeed.

Adventure

70. Those who praise the adventurous spirit fail to consider the criminals among us.

Adversary

71. Our greatest adversary in life can be our lack of will to succeed.

Adversity/Prosperity

72.　Adversity challenges all we hold dear,
reveals friends and foes with all the sear
of fires burning everything in sight.
Oh, return us to prosperity's clueless night.

73.　Adversity exposes the stranger within.

74.　Adversity is education, whereas prosperity is
seduction.

75.　Adversity shared brings a prosperity of friends.

76.　Adversity strips away our pretenses, leaving
nothing but who and what we are.

77.　Considering our fate, I am inclined to prefer the
pointless pleasures of prosperity to the creative
agonies of adversity.

78.　Few can endure prolonged prosperity without
succumbing to self-importance and disdain for
those less fortunate.

79.　In this world, doing the right thing rarely avoids
censure.

80.　Perhaps we are encouraged to praise adversity
because it is unavoidable.

81.　Prosperity conceals our flaws, and adversity tests
our character.

82.　Prosperity favors pride over humility.

83. Prosperity is always in jeopardy, for the cost of living is as reliable as the morning sun, always rising.

84. Prosperity reaches deep within
to find one's very favorite sin.

85. There are lessons that can be taught only by adversity.

86. When all seems to go awry,
no way to make things right,
some bend with a woeful sigh
while others choose to fight.
All face the dreadful night.

Advertisement

87. Advertising defines cultural values with the precision of a catechism.

88. Advertising hopes to program consumption without the interference of critical thought.

Advice

89. Even the devil can deliver good advice.

90. Experience advises without compassion.

91. Fear advises from a position of strength.

92. Good advice is the easiest to ignore since it is the hardest to implement.

93. If the wealthy are wise, they will emulate the poor by walking more and eating less.

94. It is a compliment to ask advice and dangerous to give it.

95. It is safer to give money than to give advice.

96. Those who take good advice are as able as those who don't need it.

97. When we give advice, we define the example we wish was ours.

Affectation

98. Affectation is the theater of the obsessed, where our imperfections are the stars.

99. Affectation lets everyone know what we cannot do.

Affection

100. Affection is the greatest gift of all, for it bypasses the mind, going directly from one heart to another.

101. Affection trumps praise in the final scheme of things.

102. To brag about the devotion you inspire is to deserve none.

Affliction

103. Those who see severe affliction as some mysterious blessing have found a way to endure.

Africa

104. On many trips to Africa
where feral life abounds,
went to a place the human race
first walked these vibrant grounds
where family still surrounds.

Age

105. A return to youth is never part
of wisdom's point of view;
best to remain young at heart
when well past twenty-two.

106. Age can abstain without fault.

107. Age: crime's cure that comes too late.

108. Age does not change us but seems to define us with clarity.

109. Age is a period of broad horizons and narrow choices.

110. Age strips away the posture of youth, revealing who we are.

111. Age wishes to be youthful without youth.

112. Aging: the world sees a shrinking shell; I see an expanding universe of unfinished dreams.

113. As we grow older, we are relentlessly pursued by that specter of diminished capacity and oblivion.

114. First time:
A cry was heard, seemed far away—
"Old man" rang down the street.
Seemed strange to me that one would say
what seemed so indiscreet;
old age and I did meet.

115. I am currently working on two books, putting age in a quandary.

116. In old age, I spent time with a camera and a pen, and I loved with the passion of youth.

117. In old age, our minds wander back to things better left alone.

118. In old age, the writers of the past increasingly become our friends.

119. Regrets and the death of loved ones make it difficult for the old to feel young.

120. Rejection of the new is acceptance of age.

121. Second childhood is not second youth.

122. Some are old and untouched by experience.

123. The aging process is inexorable and cruel.

124. The faults of age are particularly poignant, for they reveal we learned nothing from the past.

125. The final act of age can be a betrayal of a lifetime of thought in pursuit of eternal life.

126. The hunger for life increases with the years.

127. The inevitable arthritis of age need not reach the mind. Converse with great minds through their writings, and you will not grow old.

128. The longer you live, the more you realize that love is life's greatest achievement.

129. The old should resist the impulse to talk of the good old days and should find their way to new goals.

130. The old who strive to be young have lost their way. Age has its own strength and purpose.

131. The older we get, the more we appreciate a simple walk around the block.

132. The older we get, the more we feel the loss of old friends; they are simply irreplaceable.

133. Those who are very old love with a love that transcends biology.

134. The wisdom of age is balanced by a foolery that denies we are old.

135. The wrinkles written on the heart
    are deeper than the rest,
    for when our spirit comes apart,
    life gives no interest.

136. There is sadness that comes with age
    for things both said and done;
    we wish we could turn the page
    on pain we can't outrun.

137. Those older folks who complain about life may find solace in the fact that they may leave it soon.

138. Those who claim to have unraveled the mystery of existence in old age have kept their secret.

139. Those who see glory in gray hair
    see growing old as something fine.
    But what of those who find despair
    when many years end in decline,
    when love is left with a shrine?

140. Being old enough to know better may sadly be a reason not to try.

141. To say you look young is to say you are old.

142. Very few past the age of sixty can recognize the value of something new.

143. We feel age in the depth of our understanding. We have been there before.

144. We often learn the importance of a decision long after it is made. Why are the insights of age so often ignored?

145. When you are very young or very old, it is better not to act your age.

146. Years come and go, along with those we love. We wish we could stop the torments of time that leave wounds that never heal.

147. Youth is blind to truth that age cannot escape.

Age and Wisdom

148. Some say with passing years
they doubt age makes us wise;
but surely life's flood of tears
wash away the lies.

Aggression

149. There is no aggression like the truth, for it allows no defense.

Agnosticism

150. Agnosticism is embraced by those who do not put belief in chains or allow desire to dominate.

151. Agnosticism recognizes ignorance where others must believe.

152. If there were a God, he would not be fooled by those who drop to their knees in fearful admiration. It is far more likely that he would respect those who doubt his existence.

153. The agnostic professes ignorance, whereas the atheist and theist are convinced they know the truth.

154. The agnostic may consider the possibility of a first cause without a personal God.

155. Those who hold tight to agnosticism in their darkest hour reveal character and courage unknown to the groveling majority.

156. Those who passionately believe in anything are likely to be offended by agnostics.

157. Although agnosticism, unlike theism and atheism, declares its ignorance of the existence of a God, it shares its lack of belief with atheism.

Aim

158. There is joy in trying a number of things. Lasting success is a will-o'-the-wisp, so enjoy the struggle to succeed with little concern for winning or losing.

Alone

159. Belonging is not the best way to think for ourselves. The lone wolf escapes the biases of common thought.

Ambiguity

160. Ambiguity encourages more than one point of view.

Ambition

161. Ambition rarely seeks unrecognized excellence, however sweet.

162. Ambition sees a single star in the sky.

163. Ambition to do very well
without desire for fame
is rarer than a ne'er-do-well
who wins a famous name.

164. Seek power and find a soul in chains,
      self lost when ambition reigns.

165. The more we desire to appear great, the smaller
      we become.

166. The pursuit of excellence can be led astray by the
      need for approval.

America

167. A country that invades another land on moral
      grounds appears to be violating God's rule of
      nonintervention.

168. A country where God and guns hold sway makes
      the will of the people a frightening prospect.

169. A government that reduces a person to poverty
      before providing medical care has misplaced
      priorities.

170. A political defeat in South Carolina is a moral
      victory.

171. America is becoming a corporate monarchy where
      gold is king.

172. If Iraq were a Christian country, would America
      wage war over weaponry? Where religion
      reigns, all are in jeopardy who fail to uphold the
      prevailing view.

173. If our schools embrace prayer and creationism, then all semblance of education is lost in the desert of thoughtless belief.

174. If religion is fundamental in our society, then it must share the spotlight with the advanced killing machines that abound.

175. In America, a religious scoundrel will always prevail over a virtuous atheist in the political arena.

176. In America, athletic prowess is admired far more than goodness.

177. In America, brains and money are often admired in a moral vacuum.

178. In America, candidates for public office can face anything but a critically thoughtful constituency.

179. In America, greatness is not a requirement for, but an obstacle to, becoming president.

180. In America, self-defense has come to mean "strike first."

181. In America, the opinion of children is thought more valuable than that of an adult with decades of experience.

182. In America, those who are thin and past fifty are seen as an anomaly or worse.

183. In early twenty-first-century America, more resources were dedicated to schools in Afghanistan than to those in the United States. Apparently, charity does not begin at home.

184. In the United States, a draft would deliver a death blow to war.

185. It is considered outrageous to steal money from a dead person on the street, yet Congress writes laws to do this to thousands.

186. Of all the advantages the United States enjoys, none is more important than its racial impurity.

187. Our country of eternal war should not be surprised by violence in American classrooms.

188. Public transportation reveals the intellectual lethargy of our citizens. Very few are reading books.

189. Should a culture prone to violence have ready access to guns?

190. Since divine behavior represents moral perfection, the choice to violate God's nonintervention rule by invading foreign lands gives one pause.

191. The American people would rarely choose war if they were made to endure war in all its horror.

192. The governor of a state who thinks the American Revolution was fought in the sixteenth century should embarrass every citizen.

193. The military adventurism of the United States in pursuit of a "better world" has inspired more hate than love.

194. The royalty of the United States are actors and athletes.

195. The United States has become one of Tom Jefferson's "nations of eternal war."

196. The vanishing of jury trials in the United States represent a tyranny not unlike that which provoked the American Revolution.

197. The voluntary military of America allows most citizens to sacrifice nothing while making war as easy to wage as walking across the street.

198. Those in Congress who take a stand
    are nowhere to be found;
    fear of corporate reprimand
    brings every vote around.

199. Greeting a stranger in big-city America is seen as a threat.

200. To police the entire world is to make more enemies than friends.

201. When a US president states atheists are not citizens, he is dismissing many eminent people. This presidency reflects the weight of many votes in our democracy.

Analogy

202.   When proof fails, in desperation we resort to analogy.

Ancestry

203.   Ancestry is irrelevant; our actions define us with uncompromising clarity.

204.   Great ancestors embarrass those who fail to perform.

205.   My ancestry is Irish and German, and my writing pursues truth wherever it is found.

206.   To brag about our ancestors is to bring our own worth into question.

207.   To find your worth in those who came before is to give the dead life they have no more.

Anecdote

208.   Revealing anecdotes can capture subtleties beyond the reach of reason.

Angels

209.   When people describe angels and their powers, we realize their source is pure imagination.

Anger

210. Anger defines us, for it reveals what matters.

211. Anger is an expression of morality.

212. Anger justified by the facts
     can lead to deadly heart attacks.
     Best to retreat to reason's rule;
     leave anger to the bloody fool.

213. If profound evil provokes no anger, then you are
     simply amoral.

214. Listen carefully to anger's outbursts, for they have
     integrity untouched by discretion.

215. To bring no anger to injustice ensures its
     continuation.

Animals

216. Those who think that all other animals are created
     for humans' use will hopefully encounter an
     alien being from another world with this view of
     humans.

Anonymity

217. Anonymity is the test of character.

218.	I suspect *only* the famous can fully appreciate the freedom and comfort of anonymity.

Answer

219.	Our thirst for answers can lead to accepting the absurd.

220.	The answers that go on and on
can rarely be relied upon;
truth's vision is so clear and fine,
often seen in a single line.

221.	The best answers open a world of questions.

222.	With regard to fundamental questions, final answers end not only conversation but even thought itself. Belief blocks all treks to truth.

Antagonism

223.	Antagonism should be welcomed, for it may show us we are wrong or at least prompt us to think.

Anticipation

224.	The real loss of a loved one trumps all anticipation.

Anxiety

225.   Anxiety can pay off big when it is right.

226.   The best way to avoid anxiety is to deny the inevitable.

Apathy

227.   Apathy can be good when intentions are bad.

228.   Apathy is not mere indifference, but a prescription for chaos on a grand scale.

Aphorism

229.   An aphorism is a brief statement of truth or sentiment, remembering that truth is a moving target.

230.   An aphorist should not do your thinking for you but strike a nerve that demands thought.

231.   Aphorisms can be tart or tasty so long as they provoke one to think.

232.   Aphorisms strive to cut through convoluted argument with the scalpel of insight.

233.   Aphorists may express one thought at one moment and an opposing thought the next. Truth may be somewhere in between.

234. Every aphorist should strive, though failure is assured, to compete with Bartlett.

235. Fiction surrounds truth, whereas aphorisms capture its essence.

236. In writing aphorisms, one strives to avoid the trivial. The question is, what is trivial?

237. The aphorist seeks the buried treasures of truth.

238. The wordy expanses of the novelist become intolerable to those of us who value the lean efficiency of the aphorist.

239. The writer of aphorisms is after the quotable line, the perfect marriage of thought and language.

240. Well-written aphorisms are provocative, sometimes profound, and always incomplete.

Apology

241. An apology may be a hope that one can improve.

242. As moral creatures, we are compelled to apologize.

243. The notion that apology is egotistical may on occasion be true, but it is still admission of error.

Appearances

244.   Appearance is a valid guide
       for animals far and wide
       except for man's Jekyll and Hyde.

245.   Appearances we promote
       for acceptance far and wide.
       Seems better to do our best
       and find no need to hide
       the fact we truly tried.

246.   Appearances are the world's measure of who we
       are. Even the best of us need a facade.

247.   Beard and baldness lay no claim
       to the brains we seek;
       must look deeper for the flame
       of wisdom's deep critique.

248.   One's appearance is persuasive, though it is
       nothing more substantial than symmetry.

249.   The prude may be a lecher in disguise.

250.   We seek to make things appear
       what they are simply not;
       few deceived by the veneer
       of this unseemly plot;
       will not change our lot.

251.   When alone we are true to one
       buried deep inside;
       with others we are fiction spun
       to please both far and wide—
       seems there is much to hide.

Applause

252. Being censored by the many is applause enough.

253. To seek applause is to imprison yourself in the tastes and values of others.

254. To seek applause is to never deserve it.

255. To welcome applause, no matter its source, is sheer vanity.

Appreciation

256. Appreciation is the key
to every joy that life provides;
it is the way for you and me
to put away all that derides.

257. Appreciation, to be meaningful, must be limited to a few precious things.

258. Life is lost if one cannot see
the wondrous gift of you and me.

259. The appreciation of a book is often more dependent on the mind of the reader than on the brilliance of a writer.

260. Women are cherished for beauty, and men for wealth. One wonders where virtue lies.

Approval

261. If you deny your true nature in a quest for approval, you have given your life away to those who do not care.

262. If your need for approval is great, you become the critics' prey.

263. The need for approval is a tyranny that robs us of our individuality.

Architecture

264. Cathedrals are testaments to our mortality; the more elaborate, the greater the desperation.

Argument

265. Argument that seeks to overcome can never compete with a good example.

266. Arguments from authority put memory on the throne.

267. Arguments that seek to overcome, however astute, fail by way of intent.

268. Flawed postulates can bring perfect arguments to false conclusions.

269. One can argue badly and be right and argue perfectly and be wrong.

270. Perfect argument can lead to error, and simple belief can stumble onto truth.

271. The prejudice of our postulates allows us to reason our way to what we must believe.

272. Losing an argument is cause for celebration, for we lose nothing but error.

273. To lose an argument is to win knowledge.

Aristocracy

274. The most virtuous are an aristocracy largely ignored.

Armament

275. To sell weapons is to promote war.

Arrogance

276. Those who brag of being self-made never consider the origin of self.

277. To live long and be self-important is impossible for anyone who thinks.

Art

278. Art can bring new insight or dress the old in the unforgettable.

279. Confusing change with progress is pervasive in artistic endeavor.

280. Every artistic endeavor is a self-portrait.

281. The artistic quest is to be as genuine as a child and as skilled as an accomplished adult.

282. Those vendors of abstract art who convincingly speak of its creative genius are among the world's greatest actors.

Asceticism

283. Pleasure denied can bring pure ecstasy.

Aspiration

284. Aspirations are not inherently good. Blake's soaring bird may seek mayhem.

285. Our aspirations define us.

286. Seems all our strivings end in dust;
     still we love and say we must.
     We yearn to be more than a part
     of all we see right from the start.

287. Though I write poetry and aphorisms, my greatest aspiration is life with Joselita.

288. To reach for the stars is success enough.

Assassination

289. Assassination is a compliment rarely deserved.

Associate

290. Our associates define us, for the good will not tolerate the bad, nor the bad the good.

Association

291. Reading the great poets as a boy gave me more than any formal education.

Astronomy

292. Astronomy fosters more wonder than worship.

Atheism

293. If there is a God, he should cherish the atheist who confronts death without recanting.

294. The atheist never blasphemes, for he cannot offend what does not exist.

295. The courage of atheism is to choose evidence over desire and fear.

296. The epitaph:
Here lies the atheist,
dressed so well
to go to hell.

297. When someone asserts his or her atheism, the first question should be, do you deny the possibility of a first cause?

298. Although atheism is in the mind, fear is in the heart.

299. When belief in God is based on fear, it is not far from atheism.

Atheism and Theism

300. Atheists and theists are bedfellows, for they both presume to know.

Attention

301. Attention is as rare as genius, which depends upon it every day.

Attitude

302. Attitude confronted by gravity may find it prudent to acquiesce.

303. Attitude that is faithful to the facts rarely inspires happiness.

304. Since there is much mystery, why not embrace the improbable?

305. To love all is clearly absurd.

Authenticity

306. To admit error openly and without hesitation reflects an authenticity that being correct can never provide.

Authority

307. I reject authority in myself and others.

308. Resentment of authority is the inevitable response to a world where the unfit, with rare exceptions, rise to power.

Authorship

309. An author's importance is often defined by financial success, but his worth may lie elsewhere.

310. An aphorist strives to dress up the old and address
the new.

311. Frost was wrong; we don't all write for money.

Autumn

312. Autumn's vibrant colors of decline match
perfectly the creative endeavors of those thought
to be past their prime.

313. In autumn's final throes, the sun comes closer
with the chilly message of inevitable decline.

314. The autumnal leaf seems vibrantly alive till it falls
into the oblivion that consumes us all.

315. The wings of autumn seem alive
in multicolored mirth,
flow gently down till they arrive
at welcoming Mother Earth;
we hope for a rebirth.

Avarice

316. Avarice is not so bad when intended for those
who follow.

317. The avarice of age is the desperate desire to
possess all when confronted with the *nothing* that
endures.

Average

318. The average man is the stuff
of greatness we admire;
among his ranks we find enough
of passionate desire
to set the world on fire.

319. To say that being unknown is to be average is to
denigrate many private people and to imply that
fame is always a measure of greatness.

Aviation

320. It is no surprise that Tennyson predicted aerial
warfare, considering the nature of men who
are clever enough to create planes but lack the
wisdom to avoid war.

Awareness

321. Being aware that galaxies collide brings into focus
what truly matters. The trivia we once cherished
vanish in the wake of cosmic catastrophe.

Baby

322. A baby is self-interest incarnate.

Baldness

323. The curly hair of youth is found
to vanish as the years go by
and find a man who may be found
with what is seen as wisdom crowned.

Ballad

324. Songs do far more than logic fine
by touching mind and heart;
they bring to us an anodyne
of compelling art.

Barbarity

325. We become inured to barbarity until each
successive slaughter becomes a part of the ordinary.

Bargain

326. The bargain hunter often sees the deal as a steal.

Bashfulness

327. One can only hope that the bashful eventually
learn that their strategy of silence has few benefits,
whereas revealing oneself may result in a friend.

Bastard

328. Our birth may be a mystery, but our worth is evident to all.

329. Those of doubtful origin have their pick of ancestors.

Beard

330. To wear a beard is to be seen
as one with thought profound;
but listen well for a spell
before you are spellbound.

Beast

331. Man is a rational beast who finds arguments for killing as convincing as geometric proof.

332. Man is the beast who thinks deeply and kills his own kind with passion best understood by the devout.

Beauty

333. A beautiful face may show no trace of that inner grace that never fades.

334. A woman's beauty is preserved by virtue and destroyed by vice.

335. Beautiful women look alike for symmetry is symmetry.

336. Beauty has so many definitions that it remains undefined.

337. Beauty is a passport to privilege.

338. Beauty is amoral despite our impulse to be overwhelmed by appearances.

339. Beauty that transcends symmetry is timeless.

340. If you wish to compliment a beautiful woman, look beyond appearance.

341. Lies can be beautiful, and truth can be cruel.

342. No single feature brings a face
to what is true and lasting grace;
the parts must join with such sway
That none who see can look away.

343. Our contributions to what we call "beautiful" cannot be exaggerated.

344. Our inner longings find eloquent expression in what we call beauty.

345. She has a phantom's touch of grace,
gives forth her own sweet light.
Time's treachery cannot erase
this ever-haunting sight
where hopes and dreams alight.

346. The beautiful cosmos is replete with catastrophe.

347. The beautiful may embrace virtue more easily
than the ugly.

348. The beauty born of skin and bone
impresses all who see.
The beauty found in good alone
is for eternity.

349. The lovely face without a trace
of sweetness deep within
has no touch of that lasting grace
that loves through thick and thin—
is nothing more than skin.

350. The sad side of beauty is that it must fade.

351. There is leanness in beauty, where every aspect
contributes to the perfection we behold.

352. Those who see beauty as goodness rarely reject a
physically beautiful person.

353. To say that beauty is skin deep
is to know truth will make you weep.

354. True beauty deepens with the years;
time's wrinkles only show
that love endures, though drenched in tears
from knowing we must go.

355. We deeply respond to beauty when awe replaces
words.

356. Why are many called beautiful who clearly are not? Surely, a pleasing symmetry is unrelated to the worth and dignity of a human being.

357. Without virtue, beauty is no more than a gaudy display.

358. Women with physical beauty are faced with a problem unknown to the unattractive.

Bed

359. Early to bed and early to rise will end in our demise.

360. The bed can be a place quite fine
or where we must reside;
gives rest when well or in decline
for nature will decide.

Bee

361. It is doubtful that the honey bee intends to serve humanity, as some believe.

Begging

362. Praying is beggary placed on the pedestal of desperate belief.

Behavior

363. Our actions appear to define us until we look beneath.

364. Our behavior defines us. Bad behavior should be damned, whether there is free will or not.

365. We cannot turn away from the mirror of behavior.

Belief

366. A belief system is defined by the behavior that flows from it.

367. All problems are soluble in the warm embrace of comfortable belief.

368. Although nothing is certain, we should treat what is beyond the improbable as irrelevant.

369. As night approaches, reason fades into fearful belief in eternal life.

370. Assumptions not subject to change imprison us in a world of our own making.

371. Belief allows us to see more and know less.

372. Belief and behavior are strangers.

373. Belief based on reward and punishment bears no relation to truth.

374. Belief based on some authority can also be true.

375. Belief buffers reality.

376. Belief can bring a peace unknown to those committed to reason.

377. Our beliefs drive us relentlessly; they are desires' legacy.

378. Belief can bring us to our knees
with hope that life brings more
than a few years of joy and tears
that end with no encore.

379. Belief coats the corrective lens of experience with comfortable fantasies.

380. Belief coats the real with the ambrosia of desire.

381. Belief converts possibility to certainty, removing any impulse to think.

382. Belief founded on evidence goes by another name.

383. Belief fueled by fear and desire is ever opposed to tentative truth that readily embraces the new.

384. Belief in a heavenly hereafter is a blessing I did not receive.

385. Belief is held captive by desire and fear; it is rarely free.

386. Belief is more likely than truth to bring satisfaction.

387. Belief is often no more than comfortable self-deception.

388. Belief makes the impossible possible, or so it seems.

389. Belief often favors the incomprehensible.

390. Belief often finds truth an inconvenience to be ignored.

391. Belief that is contrary to the heart's desire is more likely to be true.

392. Belief that sustains us requires no proof.

393. Belief without compelling evidence defines with uncommon clarity what we do not wish to know.

394. Belief, however improbable, that assuages pain and brings comfort is not without merit.

395. Belief, if sufficiently strong, overcomes all objections.

396. Belief is better seen as a tool than as truth.

397. Beliefs abound to protect us from the dark, thoughts reservoir of hope that we impart to all who need the power of a prayer in a bleak, indifferent world that does not care.

398. Belief's role is to overcome inevitabilities and bring us peace.

399. Beliefs that contribute to survival have a utility that transcends any truth to the contrary.

400. Bias is the bedrock of human thought.

401. Certainty is born in the bosom of need. We believe what we must believe.

402. Certainty is difficult to achieve in a world created by the observer and observed.

403. Desire hones belief into certainty.

404. Elaborate belief systems evolve to overcome the threat of existential irrelevance.

405. Embrace comfortable belief with the understanding that it is light-sensitive.

406. Every flawed argument is made perfect in the cauldron of fiery fear.

407. Fear and love inspire belief.
Fear wells up - is most sincere.
But what is thought far and wide
is doubt made crystal clear.

408. Hope, fear, and ignorance spawn belief.

409. I believe in our ignorance of the most fundamental principles.

410. If all the world thought us mad, we would embrace some belief as gospel.

411. If we believe people are moral, it is likely we are virtuous and naïve.

412. If we need to chant our beliefs over and over again, they are more a wish than a reality.

413. If we need to remind ourselves of what we believe, we have reached the threshold of doubt.

414. It is true that belief in the unbelievable brings peace.

415. It takes courage to base belief on truth.

416. Many find the straitjacket of dogma more comfortable than freedom with its inevitable uncertainties.

417. Newton's immersion in religion reveals that the need to believe overwhelms the desire to discover. Great intellect becomes the pawn of hope.

418. Our will to believe is founded in our need to deceive ourselves.

419. Reality inevitably reveals the fragility of belief.

420. Strong beliefs are convicts serving a life sentence.

421. The belief in a God preoccupied with human welfare is the ultimate expression of self-importance; it is the sin of pride.

422. The comfort of belief keeps truth out of focus.

423. The comfort of belief makes God possible and truth adversarial.

424. The compulsion to believe finds comfort where it can.

425. The finest argument cannot surmount the life-sustaining bulwark of belief.

426. The improbable is gospel when it serves our needs.

427. The least thoughtful among us are the most inclined to be enslaved by ideas.

428. The need to believe is on a par with the need for bread and water.

429. The need to believe overwhelms every impulse to be rational.

430. The prediction that science will challenge religion fails to recognize that critical thought is seldom a basis of belief.

431. The stronger the belief, the less it is subject to evidentiary challenge.

432. The will to believe and desire to know are exact opposites.

433. The will to believe defines our world, not *the* world.

434. The willingness to believe is a significant obstacle to civilization. The world cares nothing for our joy and woe.

435. There is no unfounded belief. A belief serves some
      purpose.

436. There is something to be said for embracing
      absurd fantasy that ensures we will never be
      separated from loved ones.

437. Those who find doubt intolerable will rest
      mindlessly in the arms of comfortable belief.

438. Those who know the end is near
      may find their way to belief.
      Fear swells up - is most sincere
      when death draws its dark motif,
      seems too late to turn a leaf.

439. To believe in love is quite enough.

440. Challenging cherished beliefs is a prescription for
      critical censure.

441. Never fearing that you may be wrong reveals the
      power of belief.

442. Tranquility is found in the protective bubble of
      belief.

443. Tribal beliefs are the first to be challenged by any
      thinking person.

444. We accept and even seem to understand the
      irrational when it suits our purposes, but cold,
      indifferent reason is beyond our grasp.

445. We believe we are safe when we know we are not.

446.　We can share values without sharing belief.

447.　We nimbly weave facts into a fabric of meaning to support our cherished beliefs.

448.　What we cannot prove, we postulate, allowing us to believe anything.

449.　What we do not want to know defines what we must believe.

450.　I hope my beliefs are subject to change as evidence and thought evolve and are never seduced by what is merely comfortable.

451.　When asked, "What do you believe?" I am inclined to say my desire to know keeps belief at bay.

452.　When doubt is embraced,
there is always room to grow;
when sure, a prisoner
of the status quo.

453.　When millions share a belief, it is time to start asking questions.

454.　When possibility is based on belief, nothing is impossible.

Belief and Doubt

455.　Doubt is the companion of unsettled truth, whereas belief is comfortable delusion.

456.   The need to belief finds its way
to happy thought that saves the day,
while those who question all they see
are left with stark eternity.

Belief and Truth

457.   Belief brings us warmth beyond compare
while all is lost in truth's despair.
Perhaps it's best to look away
from that night that's here to stay.

458.   Brief bursts of truth may find their way
into the thought of some,
while deep belief can bring relief
to nearly everyone.

459.   The warm and comfortable cocoon of belief
should not be confused with truth.

Belonging

460.   Belonging is so seductive that for many, nearly
any behavior becomes acceptable.

Benevolence

461.   If we cannot help another without helping
ourselves, then every benevolent act is suspect.

462. Much of giving is receiving.

463. One wonders where we are on the moral continuum when we give to fill our heart.

464. Those who receive gifts galore
care little for the moral core
of those who give more and more.

465. When we deprive ourselves of what we need, in order to benefit another, we define a special kind of benevolence.

Best

466. "Do your very best" is advice given by those who have no idea what dedication is required to come close to this ideal.

Best Seller

467. A best seller, with rare exceptions, reveals that profit and performance are inversely allied.

Betrayal

468. Give me the open declaration of enmity to the duplicitous villainy of betrayal.

Bible

469. Biblical angels kill thousands in the name of a kind and loving God.

470. Fundamentalist Christians ignore inconvenient scriptures in pursuit of a personal moral code that suits their biases.

471. Granting salvation by the brutal murder of the Son of God is Christian virtue.

472. Strict adherence to the Bible would ensure life imprisonment or death in every civilized society.

473. The Bible supports such a varied agenda that one wonders how morality fits in.

474. The notion of beating "swords into plowshares" is discreetly ignored by hordes of Christian warriors.

475. To grasp biblical text is to reject the Christian religion on humanitarian grounds.

476. To oppose slavery on biblical grounds is to deny the Bible.

Bigness

477. Bigness alone is nothing more
than measures we can make;
worth is the heart we do explore
before we dare partake.

Bigotry

478. A devout sinner is embraced, whereas a saintly doubter is shunned.

479. Bigotry filters evidence to preserve the purity of its venom.

480. Intolerance of evil is no vice.

Bills

481. Debtors learn to look away
     from bills that pile high
     till that certain judgment day
     when they blithely lie—
     will pay by and by.

Biography

482. A biographer who wishes to be published must tailor the truth.

483. A biography must be ruthlessly irreverent.

484. A biography of a hero is more fiction than fact.

485. Biography dresses up for image; aphorisms dress down for truth.

486. It is sheer arrogance to say the history of the world is the history of the human race.

487. The history of the human race is replete with greatness and villainy—and the villains are winning.

488. To write of another is to reveal oneself.

Birth

489. If reason were suddenly required to promote reproduction, our species would confront dire jeopardy.

490. To never have been born would be advantageous to many. Life's scales are tilted to the dark side.

491. We celebrate birth while knowing the countless tragedies of life.

Bitterness

492. Sharp bitterness has no voice,
      silent sorrow with no choice.

Blame

493. Blame is often found to be
      our faults that we're too blind to see.

494. Blame spreads like a virus, infecting every possible host, creating a universe of victims.

495.   Those prone to blame are blameworthy.

Blindness

496.   Love's blindness makes marriage possible and divorce inevitable.

Blush

497.   A blush is closer to innocence than guilt, for real sin feels nothing.

498.   Blushing reveals a moral code
spontaneous and true,
far better than a sinner's mode
of hiding every clue.

499.   The blush of lost innocence is preferable to sin's perfect look of concealment.

Boasting

500.   A boast is a toast to mediocrity.

501.   Boasting diminishes real worth as much as it demeans those who lie.

502.   The boasts of old age are rarely more than enhanced remembrance.

Body

503. One who is always looking up may yearn to look down upon those who see only a little person.

504. Our bodies define us with uncompromising accuracy.

505. The belly is the seat of discipline; it defines us with mathematical precision.

Body and Soul

506. The soul is so illusive,
one wonders why the fuss;
the body's so inclusive,
so much to discuss.

Books

507. A book is brand-new if unread.

508. A book of thoughts that fails to offend anyone is of little value.

509. A book that seeks truth cannot be relied upon to bring joy.

510. A publisher's pursuit of wealth has nothing to do with excellence.

511. All great books have plateaus of the ordinary.

512. Beware of books full of eloquence that encourage belief without thought.

513. Books are best when they encourage thought and worst when they inspire belief.

514. Books destined to endure can be the slowest to gain acceptance.

515. Books supply much while life fills in the gaps.

516. Books that provide provocative questions and possible answers are destined to endure.

517. Books that seek favor with something other than truth may flourish in the mediocrity that abounds.

518. Books with no dark corners do not engage in a serious discussion of the human condition.

519. Brevity and clarity are the pillars upon which great books stand.

520. Fiction rarely seeks to entertain those who hunger for profound thought.

521. Great books require great readers.

522. I wonder why the anthologist creates a treasured book of quotations while rarely contributing his own.

523. Our books define us with uncompromising integrity.

524. Popularity does not define the greatness of books or people.

525. The best books enhance and enlighten experience; they shed light on life.

526. The better books are those that provoke a reader to disagree with himself.

527. The many lifetimes of experience found in books are invaluable.

528. The many mundane quotations offered by anthologists undoubtedly stem from a need to quote the famous.

529. To compare a book with other books is to ignore its impact on experience.

530. To self-publish is to be judged before being read.

531. Truly great books expand our thinking in so many ways that over the years, each read brings new insights.

532. Although those of us who write would enjoy being "best sellers," we would not confuse profit with excellence.

Boredom

533. A bore can be among the great;
we have our point of view.
Those we tend to appreciate,
common as the flu.

534. A boring writer completes every thought.

535. Boredom is a matter of intellect and disposition.
We are all bores some of the time.

536. Boredom is the dullness found in those who fail
to see mystery that abounds.

537. Boredom may find its source to be
thought so full of subtlety
that few can find the state of mind
to probe the depths of thought refined.

538. In defense of boredom: the works of Shakespeare
and Newton are boring to millions.

539. Many of the transgressions of humankind are
desperate and futile attempts to escape boredom.

540. No one is bored who strives to pen insights or
memorable verse.

541. Some who bore the many entertain the few.

542. The surest way to be a bore is to be thoughtful.

543. There are some who compliment us by their
boredom.

544. Those who yawn in the presence of great works reveal one of nature's vacuums.

Borrowing

545. To loan money and expect its return is to make more enemies than friends.

546. To not loan money is to make friendship possible.

Boyhood

547. I defined boyhood when I ran away from home with a friend, hoping to find a South Pacific paradise.

Brain

548. The existence of the human brain reveals the power of persistent trial and error.

Brevity

549. Brevity runs the risk of too much subtlety.

550. It is easy to confuse brevity with truth.

551. There are mathematical formulations and poems that rival a tome of one thousand pages.

Brotherhood

552. Brotherhood is more a wish than a reality.

553. Those who believe in one true faith oppose brotherhood with every breath.

554. War fosters a brotherhood of killers.

Bullies

555. Some would blame cowards for the existence of bullies.

Business

556. Although those who pursue the arts see this as the highest calling, one should remember that life's comforts are tied to effective business activity.

557. Honesty is profitable, long-term.

558. The amorality of business is profit.

Busy

559. The busy keep their tears away
from sorrow's deep retreat,
where what is true and full of rue
is faced with love complete,
where loss and I do meet.

560.   To be busy with love is the best occupation.

But

561.   "But" delights in tearing down all that is revered;
        it prefers the exception to the rule.

562.   "But" reduces all that we do
        to something more than bad.
        It sets us up without a clue;
        'tis malice fully clad.

Calamity

563.   All differences vanish in the throes of calamity,
        where our common humanity knows only the
        struggle to survive.

564.   Calamity can be borne or even embraced with
        belief in a wise God. The belief may be suspect,
        but the benefits are undeniable.

Calendar

565.   Events define time with a brilliance unmatched by
        our solar system's precise meanderings.

Candor

566. Candor can be proud of its cruelty, exclaiming its passion for truth.

567. Candor has no necessary connection with virtue. One can be sincerely evil.

568. Candor is best found in those
with true kindness to expose,
for the truth we're prone to see
reveals much of you and me.

Cannot

569. The inability to do something provides insights unknown to the gifted.

Capability

570. The realization of human potential can fall anywhere on the moral continuum. Those who favor enlarging human capability without qualification are denying who we are.

571. There are those who fulfill their capabilities and disgrace the human race.

Capitalism

572. Capitalism is the creation of humans, not nature. We can make it benefit the many, not merely the privileged few.

573. Pure capitalism is ruthless, and pure socialism is miserable. Perhaps an impure alliance would be more equitable.

574. The amorality of capitalism can be seen in its distribution of wealth.

Capital Punishment

575. Every country with an army believes in capital punishment.

Carelessness

576. The inconsequential is a footnote to disaster.

Caricature

577. Caricature can distill the facts into a significance not seen before.

578. Caricature sees the whole in the part, bringing to life a singularity bearing little relation to the diversity inherent in all.

Category

579. It is so much easier to respond to a category than to a person.

Cathedral

580. A cathedral reveals a keen awareness of our mortality and our desire to overcome it.

Causality

581. As causes infinitely regress, the shaky foundation of our understanding is felt.

582. Causality seeks to make existence intelligible. The dissection of cause and effect defines our thought, not reality.

583. Causality ultimately fails in pursuit of existence.

584. Our everyday experience with cause and effect prompts a belief in causality that may be undeserved.

585. The first cause, or uncaused cause, postulated by the devout is said to require faith and devotion, so that the heavenly benefits that ensue can be obtained.

586. Insisting that nothing can exist without a cause puts physical reality in jeopardy, for as causes retreat to infinity, we vanish with them.

587. Without time, there is no causality.

Cause

588. Causation is the hidden face of chance.

589. Underlying causes may explain evil, but they do not excuse it.

Caution

590. Caution limits both good and evil.

591. Caution when it comes to truth avoids the world's stern reproof.

Celebration

592. To celebrate a beginning is to ignore the inevitable.

Celebrity

593. A celebrity is one whose name is worth more than his game.

594. To be somebody in this world
      is like a shooting star;
      our blinding light is out of sight
      so soon—our repertoire
      is lost in time afar.

Censorship

595. Many censor their own thoughts to conceal that
      which is too horrible to conceive.

Censure

596. Censure can be inspired by greatness.

597. Silence is the universal language of censure.

598. What is not understood is definitely denounced.

Certainty

599. Anyone who thinks is incapable of certainty, and
      anyone who is certain is incapable of thought.

600. Certainty is confined to mathematics; everything
      else is subject to interpretation.

601. Certainty is embraced by all
who need to believe.
Doubt is the stern protocol
that will not deceive
with hopes that relieve.

602. If you require certainty for happiness, your life is
an empty show.

603. Opinion is only true
when it is full of doubt.
Sureness is the residue
when reason is left out.

604. Since we are ignorant of the essential nature of
reality, we feel free to postulate a multitude of
certainties.

605. The deeper we investigate,
the less we know for sure.
Certainty is a featherweight,
a thoughtless amateur.

606. The deeper we look, the less certainty we see.

607. The less we admit we know, the more certain we
can be.

608. To say nothing is certain is uncertain.

Chance

609. Chance invades all aspects of life, including the
thoughts of an aphorist.

610. Chance is the name we give to the inscrutable subtleties of the causal chain.

611. Everything is a matter of chance, for nature and nurture are beyond our control.

612. We applaud hard work, not realizing that this too is the product of chance.

613. The chilly hand of chance
favors the very few.
Nature's uncaring laws
let some survive the flu.

614. The despotism of chance is pure indifference.

615. Those who insist that belief in chance reveals ignorance have faith in a rational universe.

616. 'Tis strange that we often worship
those among us who prevail
while the vast majority
only face travail.

617. We do not deny causality when we speak of chance.

618. What we call chance is cause-and-effect beyond our knowledge or control.

619. Why are the favorites of fortune held in such high esteem?

Change

620. Change has its unchangeable themes.

621. Change is the stuff of living breath
no constancy survives,
the only stillness found in death
where no one ever strives—
evolve with daring lives.

622. Cosmological change puts meaning in jeopardy.

623. Have those who preach that we must change
changed their nature?

624. I prefer a changeless state of perfect love, if only
this were possible.

625. No one who loves can embrace change.

626. Nothing alive remains the same. Even love grows
stronger each day or perishes in quiet indifference.

627. Our unchanging nature is seen in the way we
settle disputes with war.

628. Resistance to change is good when evil is
spreading through the land.

629. The change from rhythmic beauty to chaos in
poetry is applauded by those who uncritically
embrace the new.

630. Those who celebrate change have never loved.

631. We cherish unchangeable love, and then we die.

Character

632.   Character is defined by deeds, not creeds.

633.   Greatness can enthrall or offend.

634.   Learning without an emphasis on character is a prescription for chaos on a grand scale.

635.   The expectation of reward or punishment puts character in jeopardy. We should do the right thing because it is the right thing to do.

636.   The pious confuse character with behavior based on fearful belief.

637.   To say character rises only from the fear of God and his judgment is to say it cannot be freely chosen.

638.   We have character when we treat others with kindness that transcends expediency.

639.   When we act off the cuff, our character is laid bare.

Charity

640.   Living charity may be a bid for gratitude or recognition, and posthumous charity is at times thought to be the selfishness of those who would part with nothing when alive. There is a dark side to everything we do.

641.   We help ourselves by helping others.

Charm

642. Charm knows nothing of "no."

643. Charm is a performance where one hungers for approval.

Cheerfulness

644. The cheerful see the best of things
    in a world on the brink,
    let troubles vanish on the wings
    of hopes and dreams that shrink
    from those who stop and think.

645. The penchant to see the best in everything brings happiness that truth denies.

Childhood

646. Childhood is something to be outgrown, not something to return to.

647. Every adult is driven by the small, defenseless, all-powerful child within.

Children

648. Parents often see early signs of genius in their children while rarely looking for virtue.

649.	The tragedy of the good child is that he or she is largely ignored.

650.	We speak well of an adult who retains the heart of a child, while forgetting that childhood is pure self-absorption.

Choice

651.	After careful examination of evidence concerning free will, can we decide that choice is impossible?

652.	Freedom is lost in the chains we make.

653.	Genes, nature's inescapable programmers, effectively challenge the notion of free will.

654.	Human beings may find choice to be a dangerous alternative to natural selection. We may decide to bring a species to extinction, and that species may be us.

655.	If there is no choice, there are no regrets.

656.	Humankind is programmed with choice. Freedom may be its fatal flaw.

657.	No species can decide not to live, save humans.

658.	Once we choose, thought is deposed.

659.	Our choices cannot escape our biology.

660. The choice to say we do not know
is thoughtful to the core,
for we see the afterglow
of a metaphor—
what seems and nothing more.

661. The more mistakes we dare to make, the more we
live.

662. The subtlety of our programming makes choice
seem possible.

663. Those who say they have no regrets must be strict
determinists or believe in their own infallibility.

664. We choose to search for truth or adopt belief, and
belief usually prevails.

Christ

665. A good person's life outweighs the mythology that
abounds.

666. Give me Christ of wisdom fine
to bring right to the fore.
No need to talk of Christ divine;
'tis goodness we adore.

Christianity

667. The Christians hold four aces fine
     while others have no hand;
     they see their fate with the divine,
     praised for their righteous stand—
     mere goodness contraband.

668. Those who proudly announce they are Christians
     usually prefer life with killing to death without.

Christmas Card

669. The Christmas card returned by post
     is what we truly fear the most.
     Dreadful loss is here to stay;
     the more we love, the more we pray.

Church

670. An untaxed church is part of government by
     virtue of support.

671. Every church is an affirmation of our mortality,
     where spires reach skyward with hope.

672. The larger the church, the greater the fear and the
     more desperate the plea for salvation.

Circumstances

673. Asteroids may come in the night,
     revealing who we are,
     a fragile species full of fright
     who saw themselves a star.

674. Circumstances reveal the limits of prudence.

675. Circumstances shape our lives through resistance
     or acquiescence.

676. Passion knows no insurmountable circumstances.

677. To hope for the right circumstance
     is rarely found to be
     more than a simple game of chance
     that ends in misery.

Citizenship

678. Citizenship is a burden few are willing to bear.
     It is not uncommon to find candidates without
     character and votes without thought.

679. Good Christians cannot be good citizens, for in
     times of war, they will not kill or support those
     who do kill.

City

680. The anonymity experienced in a large city is not without merit.

Civilization

681. Civilization enhances our ability to express our nature, which means, among other things, that we no longer need to fight with stones and clubs.

682. So long as *Homo sapiens* are wise in name only, we are doomed.

Clarity

683. Lack of clarity is sometimes seen as subtlety beyond our grasp.

684. With clarity of thought and expression, the thinker tackles topics that are not so clear.

Class

685. The thinking class weaves its way through society, careful to conceal its true identity.

686. We are put in a class and disposed of with the easy indifference of a casual aspersion.

Cleanliness

687. The mysterious connection between cleanliness and godliness makes one wonder where virtue belongs.

Clergy

688. Death assures clergy lifelong work.

689. Death puts life on sale.

690. The clergy build their flock with all the zeal of money men out for the next big deal. Find members of another flock fair game; just sign the dotted line in God's name.

691. Clergy maintain their position of respect when fear overwhelms any impulse to think rationally.

692. The gold mine of eternal life is continuously mined by the clergy.

Cliché

693. A cliché reduces life to a few familiar words, making thought unnecessary.

Commandments

694. Commandments are for those without character.

Commerce

695. An educated populace not subject to marketplace seductions would surely precipitate a recession.

696. Commercial considerations that involve pleasing the crowd, with no concern for excellence, settle for the lowest common denominator of endeavor.

Commitment

697. All commitments ultimately end in the pyrotechnics of cosmology.

698. Commitment to doing things well seems admirable till we consider those who do their best to do their worst.

Common Sense

699. Common sense can transcend deep understanding by allowing us to know what to do.

700. Common sense is defined by a worldview colored by the certainties of the age.

701. Common sense is said to be held by many and found to be possessed by few.

702. Common sense speaks of what we have least and need most.

703. If common sense were common, we would be at peace.

704. It is common sense to reject the uncommon sense of genius.

705. The assumption that we see things as they are is common sense, which becomes nonsense when we look beyond the surface.

706. Thoughtful disobedience is the opposite of common sense.

Communication

707. Body language is without subterfuge; its revelations are beyond our control.

708. Clarity promotes discord, whereas mutual tolerance is achieved by discrete duplicity.

709. Communication is often considered an unqualified gift even though antagonisms and jealousies abound.

710. Listening may appear to be flattery until the attack begins.

711. Listening to oneself confirms, but listening to others educates.

712. Our communications cannot escape our nature; they define us with involuntary precision.

713. Those who draw the same conclusions for different reasons are not in agreement.

714. Regretting speech stems from indiscretion, whereas regretting silence results from having denied a moral imperative.

715. When others speak, we listen to our own thoughts.

716. Whoever prevents free speech will be the uncomfortable recipient of free thought.

Company

717. Better to fight with one we love
than be alone and well thought of.

Comparison

718. Comparison creates a hierarchy of despair.

719. Comparison is often used to enhance our position at the expense of others.

720. We resort to comparison when something is beyond our grasp.

721. When the essence of a thing escapes us, we make comparisons.

Compassion

722.   Compassion can devalue virtue.

Compensation

723.   A world of beauty is most easily seen with the flawed vision of our dreams.

724.   The notion that strengths are balanced by weaknesses reflects our need for fairness in a world that does not care.

Competition

725.   An advanced civilization would replace competition with self-improvement and cooperation.

726.   Competition diminishes creativity by leading us to conform to the standards of those who judge.

727.   Competition is antagonism endorsed by society.

728.   Competition is the pursuit of dominance. We are diminished by the impulse to subdue others.

729.   Friendly competition is found only when we compete with ourselves.

730.   Our best work is done when we compete only with ourselves.

731. Our competitive nature makes it difficult to find joy in the happiness of others.

Complaint

732. Never complaining about the evil that abounds is not far from endorsing it.

Compliment

733. Compliments given without the burden of friendship seduce us with sincerity.

734. The compliments we would cherish, we may never hear.

735. To compliment others is to compliment ourselves by way of superior judgment.

Compromise

736. Appeasement is not compromise, for those who appease serve only to please.

Computers

737. The intelligence we put into machines will reflect our fundamental nature.

Concealment

738. To wish to conceal nothing is to be without
      shame, but not without blame.

Conceit

739. Bragging about work done does not diminish the
      work but does demean the worker.

740. Conceit is found in those who see
      with a jaundiced eye;
      perceive a privileged pedigree
      where others see a lie.

741. Conceit is more difficult to embrace when we see
      profound goodness as the measure of worth.

742. Self-deception is most difficult to combat, for we
      ignore censure from without and experience none
      from within.

743. Self-importance is a rejection of what we know to
      be true.

744. The conceit of humanity is based on denial of
      evidence.

745. Those who die are missed by few
      yet see themselves as a guru.

746.	To be ignorant of one's strength
is virtue of a kind,
a greatness found to be profound
when never on the mind.

747.	To overhear puts conceit in its place.

Concentration

748.	Concentration allows an idea to grow into a book.
It leaves the dilettante in the dust.

749.	The ability to concentrate for prolonged periods
is a major part of what we call genius.

Condemnation

750.	Condemnation can be self-serving while
appearing to be pure virtue.

Condolences

751.	When love is lost, there are no words
to bring us to our feet;
one left our side and we reside
in sorrow's dark retreat—
forever incomplete.

Conduct

752. Belief is defined with uncommon clarity when it inspires conduct.

753. Whether known or not, our motives move us.

Confession

754. Confession can be a transformation or mere information.

755. Confession is best confined to God, for all others are likely to respond.

756. Confession of evil may be no more than simple honesty, which is not to be confused with virtue.

757. A person who confesses opens Pandora's box, expecting forgiveness to appear.

758. We confess to forgive ourselves.

Confidence

759. Confidence does not create ability but sustains it.

760. Confidence expects understanding, only to find mercy in short supply.

761. We can have perfect confidence in the imperfection of our species.

Conflict

762.   Conflicts are confined to the thoughtful and wise.

Conformity/Nonconformity

763.   A departure from beauty
in an effort to create
is crass nonconformity
that carries little weight.

764.   Conformity fosters a secure nonexistence.

765.   Conformity is often maligned without
qualification. Is conformity to a principle of
nonviolence ignoble?

766.   Conformity feels the comfort of confinement.

767.   One can conform to a group of one.

768.   Rebellion is inspired by the status quo; it is the
conformity of opposites.

769.   Survival often requires the appearance of
conformity.

770.   The crowded path that feels so good
may be the best of all,
but now and then we really should
break with protocol.

771.   The need to conform changes what we see as true.

772. Those so-called nonconformists who subscribe to an aberrant subculture remain in the comfortable cocoon of conformity.

773. To be a conformist is to be fully accepted as a thoughtless member of society.

774. To run with the herd is never to be heard saying anything significant.

775. We conform to fit in and conceal our true nature even from ourselves.

776. We're born in culture's warm embrace,
follow a path few can erase;
this talk of freedom to be true
is rarely found in me or you.

777. When the fight for freedom is won, we exercise the right of followership.

Confusion

778. Confusion is the inevitable companion of thought.

Conscience

779. A good conscience can alight anywhere on the moral continuum, for our notions of good and evil are ours alone.

780. A clear conscience is often a clearinghouse where misdeeds are disposed of.

781. A good conscience can lead to genocide.

782. A good conscience is often a bad guide.

783. A good conscience never forgets and never forgives.

784. A good reputation is rarely deserved, and a good conscience is not forgiving.

785. Beware of those with no conscience to betray.

786. Conscience can embrace any doctrine with the passion of a saint.

787. A conscience confronted with the irresistible redefines what is permissible.

788. Conscience defines good and evil with thoughtless conformity to the morality of the time and place.

789. Conscience is belief charged with action.

790. Conscience is defined by belief, and fear and desire are often the foundations of behavior.

791. Conscience is fear's finest pose.

792. Conscience is inclined to deny its origin in custom where common practice is imbued with moral imperatives.

793. Conscience is relative, whereas morality is absolute.

794. Our conscience is not well-defined,
a facile product of the mind;
can find a way to kill all night
and see a God that shed its light.

795. The relativity of conscience is incomprehensible
to those who see their standards of right and
wrong as absolute.

796. There is no guarantee that conscience will
embrace love and kindness.

797. Those who encourage us to follow our conscience
rarely provide a definition.

798. Those who praise conscience without reservation
think all people think alike.

Conscientious

799. The conscientious are often seen as fools with
rules, but without discipline little would be
accomplished.

Consciousness

800. Consciousness may be mysterious, but to
postulate that it can exist apart from life is to me
pure mystery.

Consensus

801. Consensus signals the birth of action and the
death of thought.

Consequences

802. Conduct based on consequences alone is amoral.

803. I would welcome a boring world of known
consequences if only love could be eternal.

804. Those who expect logical consequences may
find the real deviates from the most perfect
reasoning, revealing a world out of touch with our
assumptions.

805. No single action stands alone;
there will be dues to pay.
In life we cast many a stone
with no thought of that day.

Conservative

806. A conservative sees a new thought as an enemy of
the state.

Consistency

807. Consistency demands that we ignore all evidence to the contrary.

808. Consistency imposes a uniformity of thought that if applied to the real world is pure fantasy.

809. Consistency in love and kindness is humanity at its best.

810. Consistency is a comfortable but dubious alternative to the damnable discord of life.

811. Consistency is not inherently good or bad; in a particular case it may be right, wrong, or irrelevant.

812. Consistency preserves ignorance for the sake of consistency.

813. Consistency, with clocklike precision, extinguishes any impulse to create.

814. For many, the comfort of consistency outweighs the rough road to truth.

815. Inconsistency reveals rough edges of creative thought; straight lines are nowhere to be found.

816. Religious consistency is seen as a matter of life and death.

Consumer

817.   To say a person is a consumer is to say no more than that there is life.

Contempt

818.   To have contempt for manifest evil may not make one virtuous, but it is a move in the right direction.

Contentment

819.   Contentment, far more than a conscious pursuit of happiness, contributes to our well-being.

820.   Contentment is a mental state;
acceptance is its core.
Whate'er its plight, it sees the light
of wanting nothing more.

821.   Contentment is the wealth of kings
who've found the emptiness of things.

822.   Contentment's ideal state never escapes the awareness that it must end.

823.   No matter what your station, to be content is to be in first place in the art of living.

824. Perfect contentment can be achieved only if we believe that everything that happens is for the best. No thoughtful person can always be content.

825. The contentment of those with little can be threatened only by a windfall.

826. Contentment with a divine will that allows evil to prevail is beyond my comprehension.

Contradictions

827. Contradictions are logical flaws that can lead to useful laws.

828. Contradictions inevitably arise from the meanderings of a thoughtful mind.

829. The reluctance to contradict another is an insult.

830. Those who find contradictions intolerable cannot be taught.

831. Thought without contradiction is commitment to dogma.

832. To dare to contradict is a compliment.

833. To embrace contradictions is to admit ignorance.

Controversy

834. Controversy fosters an equality that favors the fool.

835. Controversy rarely rests on hard evidence. It gives all views, however absurd, equal footing, which puts truth out of reach.

836. Where there is no controversy, there is no thought.

Convention

837. We feel threatened by behavior that challenges thoughtless adherence to accepted ways, revealing an empty shell of shoulds and should-nots.

Conversations

838. Being sensitive to the feelings of others is laudable and confines conversations to small talk.

839. Conversation can unite even when there are differences.

840. Conversation is inherently deceptive for it is fraught with social norms that few will violate.

841. Conversation without philosophy remains superficial, though it be immersed in the complexities of mathematics and physics.

842. Conversations are best when we lose the argument and win the truth.

843. Conversations are often soliloquies that occasionally collide.

844. Conversation that stresses truth
will often end in stern reproof,
for there is much in deep belief
resisting reason's leitmotif.

845. Good conversations challenge the obvious and end with more questions than answers.

846. In a conversation, the person who forgets what he or she was going to say pays homage to all involved.

847. Listening carefully often brings less than friendly relations.

848. Many talk to clarify their own thoughts, or so say those who take no turn.

849. Presenting our point of view can bring insight with or without a companion.

850. Talk between the sexes is full of taboos.

851. The fundamental questions of philosophy underlie the best conversations.

852. The less you say, the more you learn.

853. The shoptalk of philosophy is full of questions.

854.   We can learn much from overheard conversations.

855.   When we tailor conversation to avoid the
       possibility of offense, we are sure to say
       nothing of significance.

856.   Writing books is a one-sided conversation since
       one rarely hears from the readers.

Conversion

857.   Conversion smacks of the divine
       while doing good is doing fine.
       No need to look above for right
       for kindness sheds a lovely light.

Convictions

858.   A most dangerous trait is having the courage of
       one's convictions.

859.   Conviction is discussion with oneself.

860.   Convictions are often lies dressed up in elaborate
       argument.

861.   Convictions reside in a mental prison where
       thought is replaced by dogma.

862.   The most dangerous among us are convinced they
       are right.

Cooking

863.   Cooking rarely includes a recipe for health.

Cosmos

864.   Beyond the distant galaxies
at the edge of all we know,
could it be reality
sheds light where none can go?
None privy to the show.

865.   Cosmology combs the night sky
for what will come to be.
Finds everything that lives must die
in stark reality—
so much for you and me.

866.   Cosmology recounts the many paths to oblivion.

867.   Even God is no answer
to the universe we see,
for causes retreat
to infinity.

868.   From Saturn we can faintly see
a soft blue world in the night sky;
I wonder if we'll live to be
star travelers before we die.

869.   Hypothesis: the meandering black holes devour
everything in their path, giving rise to new
universes, and life goes on.

870. The Bible had it right when it comes to
cosmology: the more we know, the more we
grieve.

871. The universe we spy so well
is wondrous to behold.
We wonder why stars in the sky
are there to be extolled—
pure mystery untold.

872. The moon's face proclaims an undeniable
certainty; the asteroids are coming.

873. The universe is everything that exists, and
existence is ever a mystery.

874. We're part of the world of vibrant life
in galaxies galore.
We search the sky and wonder why
we're on this wondrous shore
of ever, evermore.

875. We search for meaning of it all,
a reason for the wondrous show.
Seems nothing but a splendid sprawl
that is not ours to know.

876. When only darkness fills the sky,
when cold is all that be,
will a flash of light reignite
with possibility?
Hope clings reverently.

Cost

877. What appears to be free is the delusion of inexperience. Everything has a cost, though it may be hidden behind a beautiful sunset.

Country

878. A commitment to doing the right thing outweighs love of country every time.

Courage

879. Courage can lead to a Nazi Germany.

880. Courage is not in deed alone;
fear tags along as chaperone.

881. Courage may be no more than lack of foresight.

882. Courage per se is amoral.

883. Fear of war is preferable to the courageous will to kill.

884. Few have the courage to say no to war.

885. How often does courage bring peace?

886. One can courageously obey one's conscience and kill millions.

887. Quiet courage over decades outweighs a moment's valor.

888. The courage to be different is rarely applauded.

889. There is no necessary connection between facing danger and possessing virtue.

890. Those who risk their lives in momentary acts of courage pale in comparison to those who devote a lifetime of toil, twelve hours a day, every day, to feed a family.

891. Doing good out of fear is better than doing evil out of courage.

Courage and Cowardice

892. Cowardice can be virtue full of fear,
and courage can be brutally sincere.

893. Cowardice may do nothing, and courage may kill millions.

894. Few speak of the courage of abstinence and the cowardice of indulgence.

895. I prefer a virtuous coward to a courageous villain.

Courtesy

896. A courteous act may be a mere formality, but it paints a kind face on an otherwise indifferent world.

897. Courtesy captivates and conceals.

898. Courtesy smooths rough terrain,
the simplest act, greatest gain.

899. Courtesy that is purchased is something else.

900. Courtesy unreturned prompts one to reconsider.

901. If we were all courteous, perhaps the human race
would finally become humane.

902. Who questions courtesy that brightened the day?

Courting

903. The weather seldom disagrees
with courting's precious reveries—
rain and snow can only please.

Cowardice

904. A world of cowards would be a world at peace.

905. Cowardice can reveal the courage of
independence.

906. Cowardice has a painful awareness of possibilities.

907. If we only had the courage to embrace the
cowardice in our hearts.

908. The coward allows fear to create a life of constant accommodation. Cowardice is a species of slavery.

909. We need more courageous cowards to preserve the peace.

Creativity

910. An education that provides more answers than questions is not likely to foster creativity.

911. Better to be creatively unbalanced than to level life's scales with perfect mediocrity.

912. Creativity is a natural consequence of dissent.

913. Creativity is a process of making unforeseen connections.

914. Great followers are at the top of their class, whereas original thinkers are barred entrance.

915. In pursuit of originality: the giants whose shoulders Newton stood upon can overwhelm, inspiring reverence rather than revelations.

916. Much of modern art and poetry is no more than the empty ramblings of brush and pen, reaping little of value.

917. Our death is the enemy
that drives some to create;
some prefer songs of evermore
to the tenor of our fate.

918. The creative mind cannot be captured by the teacher's test, for it asks questions and finds answers not seen before.

919. The creative mind challenges what is cherished, and assumptions crumble under the weight of critical thought.

920. The creative mind may appear ordinary or even dull till it creates a beautiful poem or a new realm of thought.

921. There are times when creativity soars above current thought only to find itself in the dunce's chair.

922. There is creativity of expression as well as thought.

Credentials

923. Credentials bring societal respect that is occasionally warranted, whereas true greatness can come from anywhere.

924. Credentials often give weight to the weightless.

925. The only credential that matters is achievement.

926. There are many who substitute credentials for creative thought.

Credibility

927.   Credibility comes with the admission of error.

Credulity

928.   Our hopes and dreams are victims of credulity.

Creed

929.   Morality based on creed is in chains.

930.   When love evolves from some higher authority, it is diminished.

Crime and Punishment

931.   Burglary is an unforgivable trespass where the punishment rarely fits the crime.

932.   Crime should not be confused with immorality, for some laws should be broken.

933.   Criminality is defined by societal priorities that may ignore moral imperatives.

934.   Punishment, as practiced, smacks more of revenge than of rehabilitation.

935. Punishment leads to self-control, not self-improvement.

936. Punishment makes one wily while hopefully teaching others the wisdom of restraint.

937. Punishment may not reform, but it serves to inform those who are inclined to act badly.

938. Should society support a criminal for life who engaged in unspeakable acts of evil?

939. The clever criminal finds the police preference for Occam's razor advantageous.

940. The guilty use due process to their advantage, and the innocent can be manipulated for a conviction.

941. The prosecutor's focus on winning makes the death penalty a dangerous proposition.

942. The small crimes that inevitably precede great ones should be seen as great.

943. Victims of crime are not concerned with premeditation or intent; behavior is all they see.

944. Those most opposed to the death penalty have the least experience with profound evil.

945. Those who condemn punishment take the high road to lawlessness.

946. Those who kill innocents and are certainly guilty should not look forward to three meals a day and the tender care of a physician.

947. Those who oppose prisons have never encountered a vicious human predator on the prowl.

948. Those who prosecute crime see winning as more important than sinning.

949. We encourage crime by shorter sentences and fewer convictions. To be merciful toward crime is to ensure its continuation.

950. When crime is profound and guilt is certain, do mercy and forgiveness honor the victims?

Criticism

951. A critic's approval removes all doubt of one's mediocrity.

952. A friend who gives just criticism of mediocre work is rare indeed.

953. A public whose view of creative work is defined by some higher "authority" is thoughtless.

954. A purely objective criticism of an artistic endeavor is impossible.

955. If you seek critical acclaim, subtlety should be kept within limits.

956. If your work is not maligned, it surely has little merit.

957. No matter how brilliant the work, it is unlikely we will praise those with whom we have profound disagreement.

958. Since critics are rarely gifted, one should not be surprised by praise of mediocrity or by bewilderment or envy in the presence of greatness.

959. Some delight in finding faults among peaks of greatness.

960. The act of criticism should be founded on what rarely exists: the artistic achievement of the critic.

961. The critic who speaks of the tyranny of rhyme is admitting shortcomings.

962. The critic's malevolent nature is epitomized by Oscar Wilde's condemnation of the perfect verse of Pope.

963. The moment one responds to a critic, one lends credence to the criticism.

964. The points of harsh criticism can be a writer's greatest strength.

965. The standards of criticism are flexible and mysterious.

966. There is consensus that critics have failed in the arts and yet presume to excel in the art of criticism.

967. There is skill in making the worthy appear unworthy.

968. Those who choose to criticize
are rarely found to realize.

969. When confronted with excellence, some conceal
their envy behind a cloak of constructive
criticism.

Crowds

970. Be part of crowds and find that blame
is spread so thin that little shame
finds residence within.

Cruelty

971. Can it be that cruelty commands our attention
because it resonates with impulses that have
contributed to our survival?

972. One could argue with much evidence that to be
human is to be cruel and that one who is always
kind is inhuman.

973. The impulse to cruelty is uniquely human.

974. The self-righteous become cruel when they never
tell a lie.

975. When people come to play, cruelty will have
its say.

Culture

976. Culture writes its indelible message on our tabula rasa, capturing us for life.

977. We think and feel within the confines of culture.

Cunning

978. Cunning is the dark side of ingenuity, amoral in pursuit of some advantage.

Curiosity

979. Curiosity finds fissures in the finely crafted facade of established truth.

980. Much of curiosity is meddling.

981. The satisfaction of our curiosity can be evil when it brings pain to others.

982. Without questions and doubt, we are barely alive.

Custom

983. Custom allows everything that it once condemned; it is time's moral compass.

984. Customs are imbued with consensual validation, whereas laws lie in wait to seize their prey.

985. Custom can make illness appear healthy.

986. Custom defines the acceptable.

987. Custom embraces prevalence as its absolute standard of morality. Choice is not an option.

988. Custom has supported every conceivable position with conviction born of repetition.

989. Custom is merely a modus vivendi that is self-sustaining.

990. Custom is the freedom to conform.

991. Custom knows nothing of timeless truth.

992. Custom says we are free to do
    what most see fine indeed;
    but once we challenge some taboo,
    our chains cause us to bleed.

993. The comfortable chains of custom give the illusion of choice.

994. There is mutuality
    that custom feeds upon,
    a practice with longevity
    that seems to be dead on—
    a thoughtless marathon.

995. Unwritten laws reach far beyond the state;
    custom rules with the finality of fate.

Cynic

996.   A cynic wearing rose-colored glasses sees only thorns.

Dancing

997.   Dance is the ultimate athleticism without the crass competition of sport.

998.   Dancers translate grace of movement into art.

Danger

999.   Danger is often first seen at the last moment.

1000.   Mortal danger redefines the possible.

Darkness

1001.   One is enlightened who sees the darkness that abounds.

1002.   Seeing too clearly brings a darkness unknown to the blind.

1003.   When darkness overtakes, we begin to see the light.

Day

1004. Beyond survival, if your day has a price, you give life little value.

1005. Nothing can rival this day of life and love.

Daydreams

1006. Our daydreams of joy would often be sheer dread if they came to be.

1007. To win a prize is fine indeed
if nothing need be done;
but to stand up before a crowd
and speak of what is won—
a nightmare brightly spun.

Death

1008. Adam is seen by some as
the savior of the race,
peace found when we succumb,
pain gone without a trace.

1009. Death can be predicted but never experienced.

1010. Death is a sleep from which we may awake;
no one returns suggesting we partake.

1011. Death is a horrible disappearance when we love.

1012. Death is beyond our philosophy; it is that hideous reality that remains inconceivable till it occurs.

1013. Death is life's answer to the intolerable.

1014. Death keeps hope alive.

1015. Death's terror is eternity without my love.

1016. Fear of death can be advantageous, allowing us to happily endure a difficult life.

1017. Fear of death may save your breath and leave life in the doldrums.

1018. How can death, which captures not only people but planets, galaxies, and perhaps universes, give meaning to life?

1019. If she were to go, it would take all my life, for without her there is no more than the pointless pounding of a broken heart.

1020. It is sad to note that few who die inspire grief.

1021. My dear friend's death made passing more meaningful than before. The finality of this horror weaves its way into daily thought.

1022. Religion's cogent argument is death.

1023. Remembering those who die,
some see as life restored;
it seems this pleasant lie
is all we can afford
when all has gone awry.

1024. The loss of a dear friend is seen as humanity in decline, never to be restored.

1025. The more we fear death, the less we believe in immortality.

1026. The notion that goodness diminishes the sting of death appears to convince few on the path to vice.

1027. The prospect of death is the birth of belief.

1028. The person who commits suicide must dread the possibility of an afterlife.

1029. The tears that come with death
may flow from love profound
or fear for our last breath
that haunts both low and crowned.

1030. The thought of death does not come home
till those we love succumb;
then we must face a catacomb
of loss we can't outrun.

1031. They say the good die young, for we never get enough of what they have to offer.

1032. Those we lose bring death before our time.

1033. To see death as the greatest good
is fear devoutly understood
by those who deny what they see
in pursuit of eternity.

1034. To the young, death is not yet probable.

1035. We cherish life because of love,
no other path for me;
death comes one day, whisks us away
to stark eternity.

1036. When a dear friend dies, one's mortality looms
large.

Debt

1037. The burden of debt is far greater than the
deprivations required to avoid it.

Deception

1038. Artful concealment is the foundation of more
than one great reputation.

1039. Carefully chosen self-deception can sustain us
more comfortably than cold indifferent truth.

1040. Deceive your doctor, and give death
a way to find your last breath;
deceive your lawyer, and the law
will find a way to gnaw and gnaw.
We find the truth is more than fine
when life and limb are on the line.

1041. Much belief is self-deception.

1042. The salve of deception has saved many human
relationships.

1043. There are times when benign deception is preferable to painful truth.

1044. We welcome deception when faced with a loss of hope.

Decision

1045. Important decisions require that we reflect on who we are and what we need beyond the roster of pros and cons.

Deeds

1046. A single lovely deed puts the best words in proper perspective.

1047. Deeds reveal life, whereas words imprison thought.

1048. Good deeds are quickly laid to rest when one bad act is manifest.

1049. Promises are our best intentions, but deeds reveal who we are.

1050. There are deeds that can bring a vacuous throng to a state of reverent silence.

Defeat

1051. Defeat is the best form of encouragement.

1052. To those who never admit defeat: denying defeat
before a firing squad does not delay its arrival
unless your goal is to die.

Defense

1053. A country first in defense can safely embrace the
irrational.

Deference

1054. Deference confers respect with the subtlety of a
sigh.

1055. Deference defines *us* more than its object.

Definition

1056. Good and bad, right and wrong, beautiful and
ugly are poles of perpetual dispute.

1057. Precise definitions clarify highlights and intensify
differences in philosophy and religion.

1058. Since science is prone to precise definitions and methods, dispute over its tentative conclusions is diminished.

1059. The more we know about something, the more difficult it is to define.

1060. Those who say our basic ideas are in agreement when we use precise definitions have never discussed religion.

1061. What is life? Definition requires limits that life is reluctant to supply.

Deformity

1062. Deformity can inspire precision unseen before.

Delay

1063. Delay succeeds even when it fails, for it gives wisdom.

Delight

1064. Since we seldom celebrate the good fortune of our friends, we are encouraged to believe that their misfortune would not be a disappointment.

Delusion

1065. Delusions sustain us, for they are a personal reality we must embrace.

Democracy

1066. A conversation with a typical voter makes one long for a benevolent dictator.

1067. A democracy at war loses its identity.

1068. A democracy that provides the freedom to seek work that does not exist has failed.

1069. Democracy claims to express the will of the people, but in the United States it is difficult to lure half of them to the polls.

1070. Democracy embraces mediocrity with the weightless vote of a majority.

1071. Democracy fosters freedom of speech and slavery to the will of the majority.

1072. Democracy in the United States reflects the will of a minority who are willing to vote.

1073. Democracy is more prone to competition than to cooperation.

1074. Democracy's fondness for mediocrity can be seen in many of its public officials.

1075. Democracy should require every citizen to make a decision. The vote should be mandatory.

1076. Democratic candidates who appear to reflect the mediocrity of the masses often rise to power.

1077. If we were to weigh votes according to the intelligence of the voter, the results could be disastrous, for intelligence is amoral.

1078. The fundamental problem of democracy is finding hundreds of representatives who will put the welfare of the entire society above personal advantage.

1079. The petty self-interest of the voter is democracy's fatal flaw.

1080. Those of modest means who vote to make the rich even richer put democracy in a quandary.

1081. When the dollar votes, the people lose.

Dependency

1082. The strongest are in need of help.

1083. The very rich and very poor fall prey to dependency.

Deprivation

1084. To want nothing is inconsolable.

1085. Old age is deprivation by default.

1086. We appreciate that most which is lost.

Desire

1087. Desire expires on the deathbed of fulfillment.

1088. Desire is a vital sign.

1089. Desire is the heart of mental life; it pumps the blood of purpose.

1090. Desire sustains and frustrates; it is life in action.

1091. Our desires sometimes destroy us and always define us.

1092. The fact that what we desire is beyond our control does not justify the evil we do.

1093. The idea "to desire less is to have more" is easy to say but difficult to embrace in a world where wealth is the measure of worth.

1094. What we desire can be far more dangerous than what we fear.

1095. When basic needs are satisfied, desire must feed on fancy.

Desire and Truth

1096. Our deepest desires put truth in jeopardy.

Desolation

1097. Old age pays dearly for its stay,
for those we love must go;
no way to chase the pain away
for loss is all we know
while tears of love bestow.

1098. Some love so well they cannot bear
to see another go.
All life is gone in grim despair
without love's wondrous glow;
can't live with what they know.

Despair

1099. Despair docks at the end of life's journey.

1100. There is despair in the realization that our
improbable existence is as temporary as a summer
storm. To embrace this despair is to choose truth
over the wishful fantasies of unwarranted belief.

Desperation

1101. We postulate an immortal soul and eternal life in a desperate attempt to deny the oblivion that confronts us all.

Destiny

1102. Congenital impulses are not amoral simply because they are beyond our control.

1103. I began writing in old age with no other purpose than to pen my thoughts. This dedication to writing came as a surprise and may be part of what we call destiny.

1104. If our DNA is our destiny, then to applaud our efforts is to pay homage to nature.

1105. It is difficult to be blind to the future in a world of colliding galaxies and wandering black holes.

1106. It is either destiny or choice; one cannot have it both ways.

1107. Our hopes and dreams wind their way to oblivion.

1108. The present can drive us to create what a certain future will never see.

1109. The winners reject destiny, whereas the losers embrace it—so much for critical analysis.

1110. Those who encourage all of us to follow our destiny ignore the monsters among us.

Determinism

1111. We don't decide to be diligent.

Dictionary

1112. Use the dictionary as a reference while freely extending the frontier of meaning to suit your purpose.

Different

1113. Embracing what is different is the hallmark of a free society.

Difficult

1114. The anticipation of a difficulty can be the greatest difficulty of all.

1115. The difficult is the choice of those who enjoy the struggle, win or lose.

Diligence

1116. A diligent devil is not to be admired.

Diplomacy

1117. Diplomacy finds truth irrelevant in pursuit of the affirmative.

Disability

1118. Disability drives some to go far beyond those who are comfortably able.

Disagreement

1119. Disagreement serves us best when it clarifies thought.

1120. Thought thrives on disagreement, for many points of view may converge on some common ground of truth.

Disappointment

1121. The inevitability of disappointment must be tempered with the joy of striving, or life itself will be the greatest disappointment.

Disciple

1122. Disciples are those who have decided not to think for themselves.

Discipline

1123. Love of what you do provides its own discipline.

1124. The discipline to master a discipline is fine, but love is a far greater force in the scheme of things.

Discontent

1125. Discontent may unhappily create,
while satisfaction feels so very great.

Discovery

1126. Much of what we say and do is rediscovery.

Discrimination

1127. The more pleasure we seek, the less pleasure we find.

Discussion

1128. Discussion may not seek truth but can stumble upon it.

Disguise

1129. Bad people are the best liars.

1130. Disguises wear thin, but the pursuit of excellence, however flawed, brings accolades. Better to be yourself on the mend than an empty shell who pretends.

1131. No disguise conceals meanness.

1132. The best people are more concerned with not cheating than with being cheated.

1133. Embracing the opposite of what we feel or believe is a favorite disguise.

1134. We wear disguises that reveal who we are.

Dishonesty

1135. Dishonesty in the service of kindness is a virtue.

1136. Dishonesty is a joy to behold when it is forged by a loving and virtuous heart.

1137. The best way to deceive is to begin with truth.

Disposition

1138. Our disposition interprets fortune and sometimes finds its way to happiness.

Distance

1139. Distance is not found to enhance
what is dearest to our heart;
distance gives the perfect chance
to upset the apple cart.

Distinction

1140. With rare exceptions, the greater the intellect, the fewer the admirers.

Distrust

1141. Distrust encourages deceit.

Diversity

1142. Diversity of race and culture must be forced upon a society to bring understanding and respect.

1143. The human mind can unite the most diverse elements into a montage of meaning.

Divinity

1144. Scripture assigns divinity to man;
       life reveals the savagery of the clan.

Doctors

1145. Doctors who demand symptoms have no interest
       in prevention.

1146. The promise of longevity
       wrapped round the doctor's rule
       inspires faith for a while
       till death wins the final duel.

1147. When we are well, we may ignore
       the doctor's sage advice;
       but when we're ill, we take the pill
       and pay most any price.

Dogmatism

1148. My dogma of doubt listens to all and embraces
       none.

1149. Our truths separate and unite us far more than
       our actions.

1150. The dogmatic avoid the discomfort of critical
       thought.

Dogs

1151. A dog's devotion seems to me
affection rarely found;
in all of proud humanity
none sweet as a bloodhound
pursuing love profound.

Doing

1152. Doing defines us.

1153. Doing speaks a language known to all.

1154. If a task is worthy, then the doing is admirable,
win or lose.

1155. When we love what we do, the outcome is
incidental.

Doubt

1156. Cherished belief finds despair in doubt.

1157. When confronted with our mortality, faith is
understandable, but doubt brings understanding.

1158. Doubt brings philosophy to mind
while faith keeps one forever blind.

1159. Doubt can bring comfort in showing us we are
alive with thought.

1160. Doubt climbs aboard every thoughtful trek to truth
while faith finds solace in Scripture's prideful proof.

1161. Doubt darkens every door in an effort to shed light.

1162. Doubt is durable.

1163. Doubt is faith in our finite nature.

1164. Doubt is no more than recognition of our
limitations.

1165. Doubt, however small, provokes reason to rescue
us from the extremes of certainty.

1166. Doubters make poor soldiers.

1167. Faith sustains the many, whereas doubt educates
the few.

1168. First principles are fine indeed
for those who must believe;
the thoughtful challenge every creed
though they may not aggrieve
hope's power to deceive.

1169. The deeper we probe, the more we are prone to
doubt. The more fundamental the question, the
more uncertain the answer.

1170. The devout see doubt as the villain who deprives
them of eternal life.

1171. Those who doubt the existence of a benevolent
God show no hint of pride; they see themselves as
irrelevant dust.

1172. To be comfortable with doubt is to recognize our limitations.

1173. To be happy with doubt is to embrace a thoughtful life.

1174. To doubt is courage of a kind
unknown to belief;
doubters risk all, for they know they're blind
to nature's leitmotif.

1175. To have faith in doubt is to recognize that the deeper we look, the less we know.

1176. To question the cherished beliefs of one's culture is to dare to think.

1177. Your first principles should rest on a foundation of uncertainty.

Dreams

1178. Do we really want to know
the language of our dreams?
The self revealed may sadly show
a savage full of schemes.

1179. Our dreams are full of mystery
of who and what we are;
seems nothing but a potpourri
creatively bizarre.

1180. Paint the skies as you wish and leave the world to those without dreams.

1181. The dream ends in the real nightmare!

1182. We safely live with madness in our dreams.

Dress

1183. If new clothes make you feel well,
   then enjoy the passing spell,
   for small things that inspire
   are precious gems when much is dire.

1184. Those who say dress makes the man
   clearly do not understand;
   well-dressed scoundrels do abound
   even upon holy ground.

1185. Women, far more than men, are disinclined to
   dress below their station.

Drinking

1186. The pain must be great indeed for the drinker
   to exchange a lifetime of imprisonment for a
   moment of relief. One can feel only sadness in the
   presence of such agony.

1187. Wine numbs with promised bliss;
   the vine wraps round the truth;
   with stealth of Judas a warm kiss
   drowns one in sweet vermouth.

Driving

1188. When we drive, we discover our disrespect for each other.

Duty

1189. A sense of duty is best confined to impersonal pursuits.

1190. Doing your duty may result in contentment that brings havoc to the world.

1191. Duty can include nearly any behavior consistent with personal morality or cultural imperatives.

1192. Duty is a cultural imperative that we have a duty to challenge.

1193. Duty is dangerous because it commits without question.

1194. Duty is defined by those who bring us up and let us down.

1195. Duty is found deep in our heart;
we seldom doubt its worth.
We are told *we must* from the start
and find it may give birth
to plagues that scourge the Earth.

1196. There are duties imbued with worth.
There are duties dark with bad intent.
Each finds a way to give birth
to deeds they claim are heaven-sent.

1197. To do one's duty is to not think for oneself.

Earnestness

1198. Earnestness can lead to passionately pursuing or believing anything.

Earth

1199. If the Earth belongs to those who preserve its beauty and life-sustaining qualities, we do not qualify.

1200. We devastate the Earth while believing we are worthy of heaven.

Eating

1201. The advice to eat just enough
is followed by the few,
while many eat until they meet
one they thought they knew—
no more than déjà vu.

1202. When something is eating us, we eat.

Ecology

1203. Our human nature has become life's greatest threat, giving new meaning to survival of the fittest.

Economy

1204. Those souls earning minimum wage
find thrift their only course.
Economies rarely engage
in sensitive remorse.

Ecstasy

1205. The pursuit of ecstasy at the expense of peace is a
bad bargain.

Editors

1206. Editors would suggest changes to Hamlet's
soliloquy.

Education

1207. A book of aphorisms covering a multitude of
subjects should be part of every curriculum.

1208. A good education brings doubt to the
indubitable; self-evident truths perish in its path.

1209. A good education should leave us with
uncomfortable answers and provocative questions.

1210. A positive learning experience may be too
negative to embrace.

1211. A student should be praised for provocative questions rather than established answers.

1212. Adler writes of "education to courage" while failing to recognize the amorality of courage.

1213. An education focused on profitable work rather than the best of what has been thought should go by some other name.

1214. An education principally focused on schoolroom tests rarely inspires passion for learning.

1215. An education that fosters wealth over public welfare has failed the individual and society.

1216. An education that puts divine intervention on a par with biological evolution has failed to evolve.

1217. When I was a student, my own program of study took precedence over any formal program of instruction, resulting in academic probation and love of philosophy and poetry.

1218. Being able to read is not being able to discern.

1219. Character is to education what breath is to life.

1220. Education fostering self-esteem has failed to improve human nature.

1221. Education is best when it challenges our prejudgments.

1222. Education is often the purveyor of absurdities taken as gospel by many students.

1223. Education that separates us from the savage is worthy of the name.

1224. Experience is the most effective and expensive education.

1225. Exposure to books may lead the thoughtful student away from the established curriculum to a place where no formal test validates achievement.

1226. Formal credentials are invaluable to those with little talent.

1227. Formal education is replete with forgettable knowledge and memorable drudgery.

1228. Formal education rarely indoctrinates in support of critical thought and kindness.

1229. If only we could distill enduring lessons of experience from the schoolroom.

1230. In a scientifically advanced society, those who are essentially amoral with great technical competence pose a serious threat to our survival.

1231. Mastery of one's language can be no more than expertise in deception. Character comes first.

1232. Morality is the mother lode of a great education.

1233. One cannot withhold learning from the eager or impose it on the unwilling.

1234. Parental abuse and neglect triumph over teacher excellence.

1235. Religious education weakens the moral principles taught by imbuing the lessons with messages of fear, obedience, and reward.

1236. Schools never begin by asking what is of interest.

1237. Schools reduce students to a score.

1238. Schools that look like prisons prepare students for the real ones to come.

1239. The best-educated individuals challenge what is taught.

1240. The goal of teacher and parent is independence.

1241. The good student faithfully masters the thoughts of others.

1242. The most valuable lessons may not be on the test.

1243. The popularity of religion is a rejection of education.

1244. The teaching of mathematics has failed if does not end in clarity of thought and expression.

1245. The very best students are sometimes found to be too busy studying to pass tests.

1246. Those of us who teach cannot avoid putting ourselves into the work. Hopefully, there is something of merit in what we reveal.

1247. Those who say that the best education develops one's potential ignore human nature and behavior.

1248. To be educated is to reach for truth untouched by the soothing embrace of belief.

1249. When self-esteem is the goal of education, our flaws are seen as insignificant, and we learn nothing of consequence.

1250. When teaching is a paid position, the curriculum is tailored to conform to prevailing bias. When truth wears a straitjacket, education is nowhere to be found.

Efficiency

1251. Efficient people remind us of machines.

1252. There is cold austerity in being efficient.

Effort

1253. A job worth doing is worthy of failure.

1254. Effort has its limits and will not make a virtuoso of everyone who tries.

Egotism

1255. One way to be and feel important is to endanger the lives of others.

1256. Revealing shortcomings can be seen as remarkable integrity.

1257. Self-importance denies the inevitability of our dusty end.

1258. Self-interest dominates with uncompromising honesty.

1259. There is egotism in profound love that recognizes that the loss of another is the loss of self.

1260. Those who see themselves as a force of nature live in a universe of their own.

1261. When people ask about you, the best way to avoid egotism is to change the subject.

1262. When we talk about ourselves, we listen well.

Elephant

1263. Those who see elephants as docile and tame have never had close encounters with them in the wild.

Eloquence

1264. Eloquence inspires without the need for gestures or intonation; it lives on the page.

1265. Passion reaches for the first word, but eloquence finds the right word.

Emotions

1266. A civilized life keeps primary emotions at bay until that moment when they overwhelm.

1267. Age brings recollections steeped in emotion, for feelings are the bedrock of our lives.

1268. Emotion is a cauldron of energy that can erupt into a wide range of possibilities. We can only hope for the wisdom to influence its course.

1269. Feelings endure for a lifetime, but facts are the discernible details of existence.

1270. Feelings must be free to be true.

1271. One way to provoke thought is to challenge deep feelings.

1272. There is naïveté and arrogance in the supposition that we create our own emotional climate. We are the product of programming that defines much of who we are.

1273. To force a feeling is to assure its demise.

Endeavor

1274. The modern painter throws paint on the canvas, and the free-verse poet throws words on the page. Each is complimented for incomprehensible subtlety.

1275. To allow others to define your success or failure is not to think for yourself.

1276. Striving for approval should not be confused with pursuit of excellence.

1277. What we do best, we would do for nothing.

Enemy

1278. A common enemy unifies parties with the narrow focus of feeling wronged. The union is more situational than substantive.

1279. Enemies who do not threaten our welfare do not deserve the name.

1280. Foes are friends in disguise
for they prefer truth to lies.

1281. Our sense of right and wrong demands the making of enemies.

Enjoyment

1282. I enjoy the hours spent thinking and writing, while knowing that few will ever know I was here.

1283. The unrestricted pursuit of pleasure brings pain unknown to mere privation.

1284. To preach enjoyment without qualification is to open Pandora's box.

Ennui

1285. Ennui is blind to the blessings that abound; it is dissatisfied with the satisfying; it makes indifference a way of life.

Entertainment

1286. Entertainment of the masses
rarely needs reading glasses;
wealth is found in games galore
where thought is rarely found to soar.

1287. The entertainment of multitudes is rarely an artistic achievement.

1288. There are some who entertain with provocative thought.

Enthusiasm

1289. Enthusiasm brings joy unknown to mere comfort and wealth.

1290. Enthusiasm for truth revels in questions that abound.

1291. Enthusiasm is not good per se;
goals define us every day.

1292. Enthusiasm provides the impetus to reach a goal;
it is applauded when we approve of its efforts.

1293. Enthusiasm sustains itself.

1294. Happiness may be enthusiasm, but among the
enthusiastic there are some who have killed
millions.

1295. If God inspires the enthusiast, as the Greeks
thought, then there is much to explain.

1296. Many leaders have shown an enthusiasm we
would have been better without.

1297. Those who preach unfettered enthusiasm fail to
see us as we are.

Environment

1298. Adaptation to environment is short-term
thinking. The survival of our species depends on
environmental control.

1299. The spring of midwinter global warming prompts
me to contemplate the treachery of bloody
capitalism that holds wealth above health.

Envy

1300. Envy compliments with sinister sincerity.

1301. Envy is an admission of defeat.

1302. Few envy the dead, however great their achievements.

1303. If only the enviers knew the true happiness of those they envy.

1304. If only the envious would stop and think, the genius of Poe or Wilde did not bring a blissful life.

1305. In a world renowned for unequal gain, envy hopes for equal pain.

1306. To acknowledge envy is to draw a self-portrait of despair.

1307. We never envy Jesus or Buddha.

Epigram

1308. An epigram distills truth into what is broadly false and essentially true.

1309. The agility of an epigram makes its truth seem absolute.

Epitaph

1310. Our epitaph should find its way
into a life well led,
so none will wonder on that day
if truth is also dead.

1311. My epitaph:
The dedications of my books
mark well the place I stand.
She always knew though read by few
my love for her is grand.

Equality

1312. Equality is fairness unknown in nature.

1313. Equality is not to be cherished when it comes to
a humanity that has engaged in every heinous act
imaginable.

1314. Fate confers inequality that will not be denied.

1315. Life defines equality in death.

1316. Religion promotes inequality on a grand scale
with its emphasis on belief and obedience.

1317. The notion that people are equal in ability is
absurd, and the idea of equal treatment under the
law is sometimes accepted in principle but always
rejected in practice.

1318. There is an equality
in all who walk the Earth;
we all face death with bated breath,
no matter what our worth.

1319. There is no equality in nature or human law, for
circumstances always make a difference.

1320. We favor equality and wish to prevail.

1321. We seek and applaud equality when we cannot
prevail.

Error

1322. A fraction of truth is a whole error.

1323. Error may have some fragment of truth that
provokes deep thought not found in what we see
as self-evident.

1324. There is more strength in admitting error than in
defending what is clearly false.

1325. To admit error is honest, which at times is a
virtue.

1326. To deny error is to be wrong twice.

1327. To readily admit error is a measure of merit.

1328. Truth is seen as error when it is uncomfortable.

1329. We pay with truth when we embrace error.

Erudition

1330. Erudition: learning long held in thoughtless
certainty.

Esteem

1331. Without esteem, there is no love.

Eternal Life

1332. All you must do is die to know
the truth that life cannot bestow.

Eternity

1333. Eternity gives us plenty of time to be forgotten.

1334. Eternity is pure fear.
When time suddenly comes near,
saying—you will disappear.

1335. Eternity is pure terror, for it swallows every
moment of vitality without a trace.

1336. Eternity looms larger still
when many years go by;
some hope for heavenly goodwill
that will not let us die—
best way to say good-bye.

1337. Success and failure vanish in what appears to be
the eternity of birth and death.

1338. The past and future find their way
into our thoughts of here and now;
these twin eternities outweigh
our hopes that fervently endow.

1339. Universes may come and go,
creating local time,
while eternity does bestow
an endless paradigm.

Eulogy

1340. Eulogies tell the world what the deceased should
have been.

Events

1341. Great events inspire silent reverie undisturbed by
the clutter of words.

1342. To embrace the possible is to never rest.

Evidence

1343. Evidence is not well-defined;
false confessions have been signed.
What we say is true and right
is sometimes seen in dead of night.

Evil

1344. Every self-examination reveals a flawed human race.

1345. Evil alone finds nothing unacceptable.

1346. Evil is sustained by practice and indifference.

1347. Evil's face, so hideous at first sight,
inspires many on the road to right.
Repeated sightings weaken one's resolve,
embrace dirty dealings and devolve.

1348. Evil's strength is its willingness to do anything, including using what is good to do what is bad.

1349. Inaction allows evil to evolve through the invisible hand of indifference.

1350. Those who see some good in *every* evil are simply amoral.

1351. Time is evil's ally.

1352. To say there is much good in the worst of us is to ignore the monsters among us.

Evolution

1353. Biology rarely mentions morality, which is the crowning achievement of evolution.

1354. Evolution defines our heritage and challenges our pride.

1355. There are those among us who would rather perish than do wrong and survive. Evolution has fostered the brief survival of a moral concept.

Exaggeration

1356. Exaggeration stretches truth into a lie.

1357. It is difficult to exaggerate the evil humankind can do.

Example

1358. A bad example is a good teacher.

1359. Example is followed indiscriminately.

1360. Good examples are a shortcut to learning that few adopt.

1361. People are followed, not the example they set.

1362. The power of counterexample is seen in children who oppose their parents in fundamental ways.

1363. The sermon of self so full of stealth may fail to inspire.

1364. To follow another's example is dangerous, for no one is perfect.

1365. Words wind their way to perfection that is denied the best of lives. Advice trumps example.

Excellence

1366. Excellence needs a moral compass.

1367. The unsurpassed is more in word than deed.

1368. To say there is always someone with greater skill is poor mathematics, for our population at any moment is finite.

Excelsior

1369. Confronted by the deadly universe, we cling to hopes beyond the improbable.

1370. Our heroes give us something to surpass.

Excess

1371. A book of aphorisms comes into existence through the glorious excess of thought.

1372. An excess of religion can be seen on the battlefields of the world.

1373. Excess defines the worthy and unworthy.

Excuse

1374. Faults are without absolution when painted with the denial of excuse.

Exertion

1375. Exertion defines and sustains us.

Existence

1376. Our universe appears to be subject to the universal principles of birth and death.

1377. The endless cycles of birth and death envelop everything we see. We yearn for permanence in a world where nothing endures.

1378. The improbability of our existence proves nothing while inspiring a host of speculations that are entertaining and unconvincing.

1379. The nature of existence is lost in a maze of possibilities. We simply do not know.

1380. The tragedy of our existence is knowing it must end.

1381. There is no greater mystery
than every sight and sound.
We have five senses but are blind
to meaning so profound—
existence just surrounds.

1382. To take existence for granted is not to think.

1383. Truth seeks relations between existing things, while existence remains a mystery.

1384. We must put aside the quandary of existence to get anything done.

Existentialism

1385. Existentialism sees the world as it appears to be without the soothing salve of belief.

Expectations

1386. Expectation soars with sweet thoughts
of joy beyond compare,
while living well is what we sell
for futures where a prayer
leaves nothing but despair.

1387. Expectations are the stuff of life,
the best and worst of what we see;
our joy is future's sweet decoy
that brings imagined ecstasy.
The saddest day we drive away
with thoughts of immortality,
no sign of cold reality.

1388. Expectations deliver us from the here and now.

1389. The golden age to come is more likely to embrace the thirst for gold than the Golden Rule.

1390. There are expectations that are certain and only bring pain.

Expediency

1391. Expediency is a principle without principles.

1392. Expediency is the principle of choice.

1393. Expediency never manages to diminish what is manifestly evil.

1394. We broadly define "must" to include anything we wish to do.

Expense

1395. Expense is constant, whereas profit is always uncertain and in flux.

Experience

1396. Advice may not inspire conduct, but experience compels with gravity not to be denied.

1397. Experience brings a depth to knowledge never reached by books.

1398. Experience gives enthusiasm perspective.

1399. Experience is folly's treasure.

1400. Experience is never free.

1401. Experience is thought emerging from direct confrontation with the sensory world; it cannot be gleaned from ideas alone.

1402. Experience is thrust upon us, but its benefits require diligent applications.

1403. Experience may bring a particular event to the threshold of insight, where we glimpse the universal.

1404. Experience piles on experience, washing away lessons that might have made a difference.

1405. Experience rarely comes from school. To learn from the experience of others is as rare as genius.

1406. Experience, so full of exceptions, challenges our cherished beliefs.

1407. Experience teaches with a test.

1408. Illusions vanish in the face of experience, often revealing a cruel and uncaring world.

1409. Our education must include the experiences of others.

1410. Rhetoric without experience is a building with no foundation.

1411. Some lessons of experience are rejected by imperatives of our nature.

1412. The heart never learns from experience.

1413. The more our experience, the less we feel different from others.

1414. The wisdom of experience is in part the loss of illusions.

1415. There are times when even failure's school of experience fails to teach.

1416. Time relentlessly moves on,
       learned a bit with each step;
       seems a trying marathon
       full of life without prep.

1417. To ignore experience is to invite disaster.

1418. Words cannot capture the dynamic flow of experience. We are part of the flow and catch fragments on the fly.

Experts

1419. A specialist should be acutely aware of profound ignorance.

Explanation

1420. Explanations are inherently defensive and rarely convince those who require them.

Expression

1421. Great expression is often the rewrite of a master craftsman.

1422. The writer discovers the self through writing.

Extinction

1423. We fight among ourselves while the killer asteroid is on course.

Extravagance

1424. No extravagance compares to the last time.

Extremes

1425. Even virtue becomes a vice
when it becomes pure sacrifice.

1426. Extremes suffer from fatigue.

1427. Indifference is also an extreme.

1428. No extremes reach a perfect state,
for balance sustains all that's great.

Eye

1429. None are illiterate when it comes to eyes.

1430. The eye reads and writes with light.

1431. The straying eye says more of desire than the poet's pen.

1432. Were we the only one to see,
would we care for luxury?

Faction

1433. Factions most often ignore public welfare in pursuit of a private agenda seen as faultless.

Facts

1434. Facts either are integrated into a meaningful whole or remain bits of irrelevant data.

1435. Facts are filtered through the senses and refined by the intellect into something that may or may not be true.

1436. Facts are in the constant flux of discovery.

1437. Facts are rejected in support of untenable belief.
We sacrifice our fine intellect on the altar of desire
and fear.

1438. Facts are so factual,
they lead us to agree.
Could it be the actual
is full of mystery?

1439. Facts are subject to biology; they are
measurements of the mind.

1440. Facts become intelligible through interpretation
by a nervous system with its own biases.

1441. Facts must rationally adhere to have meaning.

1442. The most reliable facts are tied to human
perception, which is defined by who and what
we are.

Failure

1443. Considering our dusty fate, the thought of failure
seems trivial.

1444. Do not confuse failure with sorrow or success
with happiness.

1445. Embrace failure as a great teacher.

1446. Failure is often a mark of courage.

1447. Failure is successful in the sense that it renews effort.

1448. Failure or success defined by some "higher" authority requires further inquiry.

1449. Failure reveals a greatness of sorts.

1450. If you never fail, you have chosen safety over life.

1451. It is never too late to fail.

1452. Our failings plague us night and day,
strive as we may for good;
the world recalls the times we fall,
no sign of brotherhood.

1453. The more we fail, the more we try,
the more we *are* before we die.

1454. There are some adored night and day
with reverence sublime,
who have betrayed in every way
with unspeakable crime.

1455. To fail because you never try
is to leave life before you die.

1456. Failing is meritorious if our goals are worthy and we do our best.

1457. When we are young, we should eagerly embrace failure as preparation for life and occasional success.

1458. Who is to determine success or failure in the arts?

Fairies

1459. Fairies, mischievous spirits of delight,
moonlit munchkins of mysterious night.

Fair Play

1460. Fair play is nowhere to be found
in nature's way or man's playground.

1461. Nature's indifference to fair play is seen in every
extinction.

1462. The complaint "it isn't fair" is heard from the
dominant predator of planet Earth.

1463. We see ourselves as the pinnacle of creation and
expect the natural world to treat us fairly.

Faith

1464. A professor once expelled me from a graduate
course on the grounds that I was attempting to
undermine his faith. Since faith is not subject to
proof or argument, how can this be?

1465. Children encouraged to have faith are being
deprived of an education.

1466. Faith and doubt are eternal enemies.

1467. Faith based on evidence has evolved.

1468. Faith dismisses doubt as the rambling of one who thinks too much.

1469. Faith favors creations over observations.

1470. Faith finds its way in every fearful thought,
a place to hide where truth need not be sought.

1471. Faith ignores evidence in pursuit of the eternal.

1472. Faith in a country or a God requires suspension of critical thought.

1473. Faith in evidence and faith in a loving God cannot coexist in one person.

1474. Faith in our ignorance is difficult to refute.

1475. Faith in science has moved mountains, sometimes to our chagrin.

1476. Faith is dangerous for it can transform the most heinous acts into a moral imperative.

1477. Faith is desire imbued with irrational conviction.

1478. Faith is desperate for credibility when it strives to find an ally in science.

1479. Faith is evidence of our belief in the improbable.

1480. Faith is fine on Sunday morn
to socialize a bit.
When things go wrong, best to long
for reason and for wit.

1481. Faith is not subject to change and therefore is never right.

1482. Faith is the only answer to a handful of dust.

1483. Faith is the speculation that something transcends all experience.

1484. Faith provides life-sustaining tenets.

1485. Faith rewards us, while we are here.

1486. Faith willing to change its mind
is blasphemy well-defined.

1487. Faith full of unwarranted belief has managed to seduce millions.

1488. Faith, wrapped in the warmth of desire, finds belief preferable to painful possibilities.

1489. Faith's fundamental beliefs are self-serving and should not be confused with truth.

1490. Indomitable faith rests on a cauldron of fear.

1491. Much of the world believes in what it must,
blind to the science some have come to trust.
The fear of death makes hope a vital part
of doctrine they embrace, though they be smart.

1492. My deep belief in the love of one human being for another is the closest I come to faith.

1493. One can have faith in humans' march to self-destruction.

1494. Reason's failures are found in faith's portfolio, full of hopes that sustain us.

1495. Reason's razor-sharp vision reveals more than many can bear, leaving only the fables of faith.

1496. Religious faith would have some measure of merit if there were no promise of eternal life.

1497. Science competes with faith and fails at death's door.

1498. Science does not have faith in order when it observes repetitive behavior.

1499. The comfort of faith cannot be denied.

1500. The expectations of faith put virtue in jeopardy.

1501. The faithful light candles of hope
while reason gives knowledge new scope.
The candles of hope are put out
by truth profoundly devout.

1502. The light of faith is bright in those who see
what is not found in nature's artistry.
Their hope shines bright in their world to come;
they're spared the certain death of every sun.

1503. The limitations of the intellect are revealed in the creation and belief in God.

1504. The principle of faith is to ignore evidence and reason in pursuit of belief.

1505. The religious spread the word
       to feel safe among the herd;
       the more they find to believe,
       the less doubt serves to aggrieve.

1506. The ultimate goal of religious faith is salvation,
       not virtue.

1507. Embracing faith in an uncaring world is not
       without merit.

1508. To encourage faith is to discourage reason.

1509. To resist faith is to be more thoughtful than most.

Fame

1510. An anthologist must resist the impulse to include
       a quotation that has nothing but a famous name.

1511. Fame is always a disappointment, for the image
       can never match the reality.

1512. Fame is a measure not of greatness but of
       gullibility.

1513. Fame finds its way
       to those both big and small;
       by word of mouth it grows, it thrives,
       becomes a thing so tall
       beyond the reach of all.

1514. Fame is the eternal guest of oblivion.

1515. Familiarity is fame's antidote.

1516. Fifteen minutes of fame is quite enough.

1517. Great talents bring forth great admirers and great enemies, sometimes in the same person.

1518. I suspect fame makes you appear special to everyone but yourself.

1519. I try for the prize, while wishing to remain anonymous. I have not been disappointed.

1520. I write books as a hobby, never expecting or wanting the inconvenience of fame.

1521. One wonders whether those who seek fame and power are fully aware of our destiny in the dust.

1522. The Fame Game: once fame is found, your words are golden, no matter how unsound.

1523. The famous are bright as a star
       so long as they remain afar.

1524. The famous may envy those who can walk down the street undisturbed.

1525. The great poets of the past would be ignored today.

1526. The great who live without a name
       consigned to the hall of fame
       must abound in humankind
       for many deeds remain unsigned.

1527. The thousands who held Hitler in high regard reveal the flimsy fabric of fame.

1528. The trivial outpourings of the famous are seen as a triumph.

1529. There is the dark side of fame, the infamy that never dies.

1530. Those who pursue fame seek a pause on the path to oblivion.

1531. Desiring anonymity is the wisdom of fame.

1532. To suddenly be seen as great
is to find many full of hate—
so much for fame's proud checkmate.

1533. When a good but unknown person dies, no one notices; but when the famous die, the loss is inestimable.

1534. When those reputed to be brilliant make absurd remarks, fame's aura wraps round them.

1535. Worth should not be confused with fame;
the limelight has its share of shame.

Familiarity

1536. Familiarity brings comfort that discourages critical analysis.

1537. Familiarity slides along the continuum from right
to wrong with the ease of turning off a light.

1538. The familiar becomes a friend
that may be dark and deep;
we find a way to defend
what makes the whole world weep—
as though we were asleep.

1539. The familiar weaves its way
to acceptance on all fronts;
beauty no longer holds sway
and no ugliness affronts.

1540. The woman remains a goddess so long as you
adore her in the morning before coffee.

Family

1541. A family can be united in pursuit of evil. Family
solidarity does not ensure virtuous conduct.

1542. Blood demands an allegiance that leaves one
defenseless.

1543. Family should be defined as those we love.

1544. If my father had written books, I would know
every word.

1545. The impact of parental behavior on children is
legendary, but it is seldom noted that the fragile
heart of a parent can crumble in the face of a
child's cruelty.

1546. To limit family to DNA is to have no choice.

Famous People

1547. Albert Einstein's "religion" would be unrecognizable to those who go to church today.

1548. Bertrand Russell's philosophic meanderings are appropriate. A philosopher should never be confined to a school of thought.

1549. Bill Maher should be applauded for publicly opposing the military adventurism of the United States.

1550. Byron was wrong; for me love is all.

1551. Christopher Reeve: tragedy brought forth a triumph of the human spirit.

1552. Did Montaigne's poor memory make original thought necessary?

1553. Disraeli declared that man is an angel; no doubt he would have made an exception of Charles Darwin.

1554. Edmund H. North (The Day the Earth Stood Still): civilization will not survive without a race of indomitable robots who insist on peace and civility.

1555. Emily Dickinson: the slim young girl who hid in the shadows, never tasting life, while bringing its very essence into rare focus.

1556. It is no surprise that Pope's perfect verse arose from an imperfect body. Deformity finds a way.

1557. It is surprising that Voltaire predicted the Bible's early demise, considering eternal life is at stake.

1558. Kant's categorical imperative is a rational principle, not a moral one. Applications of this famous dictum can be morally reprehensible. Adolf Hitler would have willed that the killing of Jews become a universal law.

1559. The portrait of Lincoln's perfection discreetly overlooks the slaughter of Native Americans.

1560. Mencken believed it is noble to die for an idea. The nobility of slavery or the Holocaust has yet to be shown.

1561. Nietzsche claims evil comes from weakness. One wonders who would not qualify.

1562. Pascal advises us to bet on belief in an Almighty, as though God's favor is founded on a roll of the dice.

1563. Perhaps it was too much perfection that inspired Wilde to denounce Pope.

1564. Reply to Albert Einstein: ethical axioms are not subject to tests but are matters of belief.

1565. Reply to Booker T. Washington: the dignity of working a field or writing a poem may someday be subverted by intelligent machines.

1566. Reply to Duc de La Rochefoucauld: a writer who cleverly conceals cleverness has failed.

1567. Reply to Edmund Burke: when good men do nothing, they are following the example of God.

1568. Reply to Emerson: a better mousetrap may be welcomed by the world, whereas a truly great book, though widely publicized, may find few readers.

1569. Reply to Emerson: Emerson's assertion that love is always returned with mathematical precision reflects little experience with the humanity we have all come to know.

1570. Reply to Emerson: thoughts not only rule the world but also, with the help of modern weapons, may destroy the world.

1571. Reply to Gandhi: the notion that all opponents can be conquered with love clearly reveals no experience with the monsters among us.

1572. Reply to George Santayana: Why are the old with their greater knowledge and wisdom thought foolish if they fail to laugh? Perhaps they are to find humor in the endless cycles of birth and death that appear to lead nowhere.

1573. Reply to Goethe: we are surely "shaped by what we love" into forms that run the gamut of human endeavor.

1574. Reply to John Keats: truth is replete with harsh realities, a place where beauty seldom abides.

1575. Reply to Louis Pasteur: prepared minds are favorites of chance.

1576. Reply to Raoul de Sales: to say "there is no such thing as luck" is to say that everything that happens to every one of us is not to be seen as good or bad.

1577. Reply to Santayana: the past will be repeated whether we recall it or not, for the drives within overpower warnings from without.

1578. Reply to Shakespeare: insecurity is mortal's constant companion.

1579. Sam Johnson's admonition to write for money subjects the writer's every word to the financial filter of profit.

1580. Sam Johnson's understanding of celibacy should be broadened to include marriage.

1581. Shakespeare: unschooled genius towers above the earnest efforts of empty credentials.

1582. Should Schweitzer's reverence for life be extended to Adolf Hitler and the Ebola virus?

1583. Some say Newton was compelled to believe
in God because he had no understanding of
evolution. If this is true, then he becomes one of
the many to invoke a deity when confronted by
the incomprehensible.

1584. Famous people who arrogantly ask, "Do you
know who I am?" have revealed who they are.

1585. The invisible means of support that bishop Sheen
treasures collapses under the weight of critical
thought.

1586. The US government confers awards on many
while people such as Ralph Nader, who has been a
force for good for decades, are ignored.

1587. Although Will Rogers and Bill Maher have found
the US government to be a source of comedy,
it could be argued that the thousands who die
in government-sponsored war represent pure
tragedy.

1588. William Blake:
Longevity is rarely seen
in what we say and do,
but now and then with paint and pen
we touch on what is true.
Blake lives in me and you.

1589. William Penn believes kings should follow God's
example, and apparently, they do. Profound evil
is allowed to exist in the presence of profound
power.

1590. Would those who have lied about Einstein's belief
in a personal God earn the respect of their God?

Fanatic

1591. Fanatics are rarely focused on love and kindness.

1592. The inability to laugh at oneself defines a fanatic.

Fancy

1593. What we see is mystery
for eyes can lead astray,
while fancy finds the sublime
in thought that disobeys
the order of the day.

Fantasy

1594. The phantoms of our fantasies
can bring joy or sorrow;
best find belief that brings relief
from a mournful morrow.

Farewell

1595. Bells toll, hearts falter, and worlds end in the
deadening silence of a sad farewell.

1596. The ink is smeared when writers see
their words face eternity;
no way to think of farewell
and compose without a tell.

1597. The worst of thoughts is surely this:
our last farewell, our final kiss.

1598. There are farewells untouched by time.

1599. There is no word that cuts so deep;
'tis fatal to the core.
Those who love do more than weep
when sad farewells outpour—
life lost in nevermore.

Fashion

1600. Fashion that brings beauty into the world should
be seen as something more.

1601. The fashion in modern verse is seen in the
effortless meanderings of mind and pen with
no concern for the unforgettable music that
compelled us to quote.

1602. The only way to deal with fashion in attire is to
ignore it as much as possible without drawing
attention.

1603. Laughing at old fashions is a measure of our
conformity to the new.

Fatalism

1604. Fatalism makes it pointless to think or act, for fate finds its way into every fact.

Fate

1605. Fate: the subtle progression of causes beyond our control.

1606. "God willing" can be heard by all
who know me very well,
though doubter true to endless rue,
I hope for a brief spell
when life and love do well.

1607. If we do well and will is free,
we're prone to say we're great.
But much of life is the decree
of what seems senseless fate.

1608. It is sad to see a loving heart consigned to the dust-filled winds of oblivion.

1609. Many make fate manageable through the creation of God.

1610. Our DNA, coupled with early childhood experience, defines us with a gravity we cannot escape.

1611. Our DNA has its way
in everything we do.
We are free to agree
with what we *must* pursue.

1612. Some do all the right things and find everything
goes awry, whereas others break all the rules and
prevail.

1613. Success and failure come to be
mere steps along the way;
there is no real victory
for nothing's here to stay.

1614. The arrogant indifference to circumstance is seen
in those who claim they are masters of their fate.

1615. The fate found in the rolling die
is life no matter how we try.

1616. The fickle hand of fate is found
to bless and take away;
some live so well we cannot tell
their lot is the dark prey
of fate's uncaring way.

1617. Those who say we decide our fate
see no sign of the hidden hand
that shapes all things that we create
and does not care where we stand.

1618. To claim mastery of fate is manifestly absurd.

1619. We argue with fate, creating elaborate systems of
belief that bear no relation to reality.

1620. When genes decide one must go early, no courage
or positive thinking matters.

1621. Works of science can never change
the fate of all who live;
our fear is wrapped in deep belief
with promise none can give.

Fatness

1622. When we use food for pleasure at the expense
of health, it is difficult to deny the manifest
pathology.

Faults

1623. It seems pointless to dwell on the faults of others
when we are all abundantly endowed.

1624. Our ideals are defined by our flaws.

1625. The critic who delights in finding faults will find
excellence unsettling.

1626. The happy find their faults trivial, no matter how
egregious.

1627. The only greatness in great faults is great evil.

1628. There is more to be gained in seeing our own
faults than in seeing those of others.

1629. To admit faults to everyone is honesty with more than a vestige of pride.

1630. We recognize our own faults most easily when we see them in others.

Fear

1631. Extinction-level events are more than possible.

1632. Faith in evidence confronts fear.

1633. Fear inspires conformity, not morality.

1634. Fear inspires creativity, and a savior is born.

1635. Fear is a rational response to an uncaring world, and if judiciously managed, it contributes to our survival.

1636. Fear is found in truth. We cannot escape oblivion.

1637. Fear sacrifices reason at the altar of belief.

1638. Fear sees the world as it is, not as we would like it to be.

1639. Fear weaves its way into thought, creating bastions of belief we will not live without.

1640. Fear's "do not" methodology embraces rules that have little to do with virtue.

1641. If you value every living breath
and love that comes your way,
there is no greater fear than death
though sages glibly say
nothing is here to stay.

1642. It is clearly impossible for the God-fearing to love
what they fear.

1643. One finds little value in a life that one is not
afraid to lose.

1644. Our greatest fear can come from our own
species, for unlike nature, which wreaks random
havoc, we often use our superior intelligence to
deliberately destroy each other.

1645. The dust that surely comes to all
brings terror to the race
that strives to escape the pall
with greatness and with grace,
knowing none leave a trace.

1646. The more we know, the more we fear.

1647. The young fear what may be, while the old fear
what must be.

1648. Those who fervently believe in heaven are rarely
without fear.

1649. Those who say the only thing we have to fear is
fear know nothing of science or of life.

1650. To fear nothing is to value nothing, for potential
loss is the source of fear.

1651. We are a species all life has come to fear.

Feelings

1652. Feelings define us with the clarity of anger, laughter, and love; they may implement but always transcend the cold logic of abstract thought.

Festivals

1653. Yearly festivals inevitably become a sad reminder of loss.

Fiction

1654. Edmond Dantès makes revenge live and teaches the power of purpose.

1655. Fiction can afford to tell the truth.

1656. Fiction has too many words and too few thoughts.

1657. The great writers of fiction integrate characters and plots with the agility of a dancing master.

Fidelity

1658. Fidelity is a mere abstraction till it is defined by what it does.

1659. Fidelity is said to be
a virtue without peer,
but faith can be obscenity
when evil and sincere.

1660. Being true to oneself
may lead one astray.
Fidelity must choose
whom to betray.

Flattery

1661. Flattery expressed before we think may be an impostor.

1662. Flattery is clearly what it seems,
a bit of blarney nurturing our dreams.
As much as we decry its crass appeal,
we cannot help but hope that it is real.

1663. Flattery is founded on mutual deception and is therefore irresistible.

1664. Flattery may be insincere and accurate.

1665. There is no harm in the courting of flattery, so long as one sees it as harmless pleasantry.

Flowers

1666. A flower's beauty is enhanced by ignorance of botany.

1667. Flowers affirm the brevity of beauty.

1668. I am one of nature's anomalies who find more
beauty in the written word than in the beautiful
flower.

1669. No rigor can maintain its might
when flowers do abound.
We thoughtlessly absorb the sight
with feelings that surround,
bringing peace profound.

Followers and Leaders

1670. Few have the wisdom to lead themselves and
avoid the folly of followership.

1671. Followers are always available, for the alternative
is thinking.

1672. Hitler would not have prevailed without
thousands who shared his malevolence. Followers
lead the way.

1673. How many leaders have led us astray?

1674. How many leaders want the audience to think for
themselves?

1675. Leaders are powerless without followers. Those
who follow are the principal actors in human
affairs; they are the foundation of leadership.

1676. Leaders promote agendas, not creative thought.

1677. Leaders who stimulate our thoughts are admirable, and those who tell us what to think are simply presumptuous.

1678. Leadership is often disguised followership that moves to the front of the line, taking us where we were already going.

1679. Leadership that encourages honesty is rare indeed.

1680. People who blindly follow often lead us to catastrophe.

1681. The final chapter in a good education is learning to be prepared to lead oneself.

1682. Leaders who tailor thoughts to conform to the whims of the electorate are publicly announcing a lack of character.

1683. The mindless followers of those who practice tyranny or wage wars make a just peace impossible. Many who presume to lead should not be followed.

1684. To follow the monsters among us is to allow the evil within us to prevail.

1685. To surrender our destiny to some leader is to be nothing but thoughtless automatons.

1686. Those who follow find a way to please power-hungry brutes down from the trees.

1687. Those who seek power over people are rarely found to think powerful thoughts.

1688. War is waged round the world
by leaders who do not consult
the many who have signed on
to follow blindly as a cult.

Folly

1689. A knowledgeable fool is folly's fountain of youth,
always ready for new misadventure.

1690. Folly is fatal when it believes itself wise.

1691. Opportunity lost is folly's special realm.

1692. The folly of the human race
has brought us to our knees;
but science manages to erase
all limits by degrees
till death is all one sees.

1693. Those without folly have never dared to live.
Theirs is a legacy of the untried.

Fools

1694. Fools reveal what wisdom conceals.

1695. We are all fools in one place or another.

Force

1696. A government sustained by force is doomed.

Forgiveness

1697. Both blame and forgiveness can be assigned wrongly.

1698. Forgiveness can bring peace at the expense of justice.

1699. Forgiveness can bring us to a place where profound evil is no longer recognized for what it is.

1700. Forgiveness is easier after the execution.

1701. With forgiveness we may seek to appear noble by ignoring the ignoble.

1702. Forgiving the unforgivable may be part of an amoral pursuit of eternal life.

1703. It is easy for a God, distant and aloof, to forgive, while those of us who lose all that we love find forgiveness impossible.

1704. Past abuse withers over time, reaching a point of irrelevancy that should not be confused with forgiveness.

1705. Some magically forgive by separating the actor from the act.

1706. Feeling better through forgiveness can be a Pyrrhic victory.

1707. To forget an offense is to find it inconsequential.

1708. Forgiving profound evil is a kind of immorality where our personal sense of well-being is placed above the unforgivable.

1709. To reject revenge is not to embrace forgiveness.

Fortune

1710. A happy relationship is the greatest gift fortune can bestow.

1711. Fortune puts reason in its place,
with plans that never leave a trace.

1712. Good fortune brings forth false friends and true foes.

1713. Good fortune favors the few without a trace of fair play.

1714. Misfortune encourages belief in a savior, but good fortune celebrates belief in the self.

1715. Our response to fortune defines us.

1716. The successful are inclined to deny fortune's fickle heart.

1717. Those who arrogantly say we make our own fortune ignore the overwhelming impact of chance.

1718. Being happy for the good fortune of others is rarer than good fortune itself.

1719. Unfortunate souls escape the malevolent seductions of success.

1720. We are children of chance.

Fraud

1721. Fraud can be found in those who say
as little as they must;
omissions often find their way
to truth we then distrust.

Freedom

1722. Freedom from fear is indifference to life.

1723. Freedom has no strings attached; it is tied to nothing.

1724. Freedom is pure jeopardy.

1725. Freedom is unknown to the followers who abound.

1726. Freedom without discipline is a kind of tyranny.

1727. Many find that freedom brings more jeopardy
than joy.

1728. One is free to pursue tyranny.

1729. Our freedom can be measured by our right to
challenge the customs of the day, by the right to
be different.

1730. Our freedom to express our very human nature is
clearly seen in the carnage that abounds.

1731. Our survival is more dependent on chains of
discretion than on flights of freedom.

1732. Perhaps there is no freedom, only the multitude of
influences orchestrating the puppetry we call life.

1733. The freedom to follow is what many call liberty.

1734. The freedom to overeat allows fat to enslave us.

1735. The freedom to worship is a kind of slavery.

1736. The moment we love or hate,
the chains of care incarcerate.
Freedom's found on a lonely shore
where nothing matters anymore.

1737. The more we are free to do as we please, the
greater is our jeopardy.

1738. The thought of freedom brings to mind
a race I've come to fear;
seems fond of killing its own kind
without a single tear.

1739. There is freedom in despair,
a place with no trace of care.

1740. There is little safety in freedom.

1741. To escape our DNA would be freedom indeed.

1742. To say the mind is free is to deny heredity.

1743. We are born into the chains of circumstances. We
are free to rattle the chains.

1744. We are bound by a multitude of constraints that
make the notion of freedom suspect.

1745. We cherish our chains, for they free us from the
burden of freedom.

1746. When we can do as we please, our very human
nature reminds us who we are.

Free Speech

1747. Free speech reveals who we are,
sometimes to our chagrin.
But few prefer a repertoire
we can't take for a spin.

1748. The right to speak freely is best matched with the
discretion to remain silent.

1749. We favor free speech till we feel its sting.

Free Will

1750. If there is an all-knowing God, then free will
must be seen as an illusion by all who believe.
If the future is known, then I cannot decide to
change it.

1751. Our freedom is found to be
a victim of causality;
countless causes over time
create a world of *their* design.

1752. Our very survival is dependent on our ability to
control primitive impulses.

1753. Our will is not so free as to allow us to want what
we want.

1754. The "I," we claim, determines all,
but can we then decry
the rules that seem to be in charge
of every world we spy?
Seems will is cut-and-dried.

1755. We must deny causality for choice to be truly free.

Friendship

1756. A friend shares antipathies and sympathies.

1757. A friend who asks for money is an impostor.

1758. A friendship founded on sincerity must be
tolerant indeed.

1759. An old friend is a mirror with a memory.

1760. Brotherhood is more a matter of friendship than of family.

1761. Friendship that asks for nothing is truly something.

1762. Friendship finds the appearance of frankness an endearing deception.

1763. Friendship forged in kindred weakness can become our greatest strength.

1764. Friendship is best when it freely reveals our worst.

1765. Friendship is preserved by recognition of the unforgivable.

1766. Friendship is pristine among relationships, for it is love without an agenda.

1767. Good fortune is the ultimate test of friendship.

1768. How fragile is friendship that finds success too much to endure.

1769. If only our friends were as dedicated as our enemies.

1770. In youth, every agreeable acquaintance is a friend, but in old age, friendship is wealth untold.

1771. Loss defines friendship.

1772. Our best friends provide the safety of the confessional.

1773. Our choice of friends finds its way
to who we are and what we say.

1774. Our need for friendship is best fulfilled by giving.

1775. Success replaces friendship with competition.

1776. The dear friends of youth are sadly lost in pursuit
of pressing priorities.

1777. The friend we once relied upon
is never out of mind;
death came one day as though to say
loss is how life's designed—
'tis sorrow unconfined.

1778. The talk we never hear at all
is truth they must conceal;
behind our backs no protocol
disguises what is real.

1779. Buying a friend is worse than gambling, for you
have no chance of winning.

1780. True friendship will not take advantage; its
impulse is more to give than to receive.

1781. When friendship is an opportunity, it is a sham.

1782. Youth forms friendships with passionate
innocence. There is selfless purity in such alliances
rarely found in later life.

Frugality

1783. Frugality can be costly indeed.

1784. Frugality is aware of limits that prodigality never sees.

1785. Frugality is rarely found in those who do not pay the bills.

1786. Frugality sees more and more
as something to deplore,
but love that reaches for the sky
is what we all adore.

Fulfillment

1787. Many thoughtlessly encourage the pursuit of fulfillment without realizing it may embrace profound evil.

1788. In struggling and succeeding, one may find more disappointment than fulfillment.

Futility

1789. Futility is seen in the endless cycles of birth and death where nothing endures.

1790. We run life's mazes, getting nowhere fast,
hell-bent on finding that which will not last.

Future

1791. Anticipation denies us the present, which is all we have.

1792. Anyone who looks ahead very far is disinclined to be arrogant.

1793. Cosmology has consigned our future to the stars.

1794. Faith confronts the future with the dim light of desperate belief.

1795. Looking to the future must be tempered by time, for eternity awaits us all.

1796. Our survival as a species becomes increasingly improbable with advancements in science and technology.

1797. Our thoughts are never far away
from futures full of fear;
love and beauty have their day
and sadly disappear.

1798. Perhaps the greatest advantage that other animals appear to have is their unawareness of the future.

1799. The dust-filled winds of oblivion wind round our future.

1800. The fear of every thoughtful soul
comes in the dead of night,
when those we love who make us whole
are seen in future fright—
we dare not say good night.

1801. The future is that period of bliss on the horizon
that makes all present joy seem trivial.

1802. We focus on the nonexistent future with its
answered prayers, while the present languishes in
our hopeless indifference.

Future State

1803. Belief in the afterlife overcomes all but the desire
to stay alive as long as possible.

Gain

1804. Sometimes gain brings only strife
and loss is found to save a life.

1805. Wanting more and more can bring
unhappiness in everything.

1806. We gain much when desire is tempered by
wisdom that knows that acquiring much never
satisfies.

Gambling

1807. A poor memory is a gambler's ablest ally.

1808. A winner who walks away
is not a gambler per se.

1809. Any patron who leaves a casino without a loss is a winner.

1810. Gamblers see chance as a friend impossible to defend.

1811. Gambling is best shunned by those with and without means.

1812. Gambling may alleviate boredom by putting one in desperate straits.

1813. House of Chance:
The glitter of light and sound
brings hope to fever pitch;
passions pulse with pounding hearts—
the thought of being rich.

1814. Insofar as business is a gamble, gambling is not a business.

1815. Many who have won a single bet believe they will be winners.

1816. Perhaps people choose games as a major interest because the rules are well-defined and skills can be mastered, whereas life is full of unexpected catastrophe.

1817. The casino is a church charged with romance.
Lady Luck is adored, so full of chance.
Parishioners play on without regret;
true love of God is seen in each new bet.

1818. The casino offers what life does not: equal opportunity.

1819. The gambler knows that chance rules but feels
fortune is his friend.

1820. The many slots and table games
bring hope to those who play.
I write verse and keep my purse
away from those who say
"this is your lucky day."

1821. The poor gamble for wealth, and the wealthy
gamble for that which wealth fails to provide.

Generalizations

1822. Broad statements are difficult to sustain, for
they collapse under the weight of a single
counterexample.

Generosity

1823. Even those who give cherished possessions to
those in need are serving themselves.

1824. If self-sacrifice is required to be generous, then the
very rich would be required to give away nearly all
of their fortune to be thought generous.

1825. We should welcome generosity even though there
are often hidden elements of self-interest.

Genius

1826. Einstein's genius brought insights to the few and bombsights to the many.

1827. Genius in writing is found in the memorable line one must quote.

1828. Genius is nourished by hunger.

1829. Genius is seeing the full range of possibilities and selecting from them what is of fundamental value.

1830. Genius is the fatal virus of established thought; inviolate principles collapse in its wake.

1831. Genius may fail because it does not display talent understood by all.

1832. Genius may speak a truth
beyond uncommon thought
or bring to art subtlety
beyond what has been taught.

1833. Genius pleases itself.

1834. Great minds see the extraordinary in the ordinary.

1835. How many geniuses are lost in the unpublished annals of anonymity?

1836. Rejection is no stranger to greatness.

1837. Talent is clearly understood,
is managed with aplomb;
genius resists whatever would
provoke us to succumb,
brings thought that makes us numb.

1838. The subtlety of genius may lead to success in the
world of thought and failure in the world at large.

1839. The temperament of genius is rarely found in
politics. Running for office rarely appeals to the
finest minds.

Gift

1840. A gift is a loan incognito.

1841. A gift with strings attached smacks more of
puppetry than of generosity.

1842. The gift of love in any of its manifestations is
prized above all others.

1843. Those who give with expectation of reward have
perverted the spirit of giving.

1844. Time is the ultimate gift.

1845. To win the gift of love is all
that one can hope for, a windfall.
No matter what the world may say,
love is the gift that does outweigh.

Giving

1846. Giving time is the greatest act of giving for it is giving part of your life.

1847. We are possessed by what we cannot give.

Global Warming

1848. Prediction: the world leaders will fail us, millions will die, and economic ruin will be incalculable.

1849. Those who dismiss global warming as a mere heat wave have lost all credibility. They clearly prefer to ignore the problem in pursuit of personal advantage.

Goals

1850. A goal reached may signal the end of a joyful struggle to succeed.

1851. If the best that is done does not discourage our participation, we have found our way.

1852. If you allow others to deliver the final word on your success or failure, you have failed.

1853. It is best not to set your hopes on the favorable opinion of others.

1854. It is tempting to believe that our own pursuits are more significant than those of others, but a moment's reflection reveals that destiny is the great equalizer.

1855. Life is enriched by deprivation that feeds our goals.

1856. Many of what we call limits are self-imposed.

1857. Set your own standards, define your own goals, and find peace in knowing you have done your best.

1858. So long as you have goals, you have life.

1859. The older we get, the more we see success and failure as phantoms that fade into the misty indifference of fate.

God

1860. A God is more likely to be feared than loved. A first cause cannot be seen, touched, or embraced.

1861. A nonhuman God is impossible to conceive.

1862. A very human God has flawed credentials.

1863. As astronomers find more and more earthlike planets and finally encounter intelligent life, believers will say these too may be among God's chosen few.

1864. As causes recede to infinity, God appears.

1865. As science advances, God retreats.

1866. Belief in God brings more bloodshed than love and kindness.

1867. God has little meaning beyond the notion of a first cause.

1868. God is complicit in all atrocities through his principle of noninterference.

1869. God is less than those he is said to have created, for in his omnipotence he is without compassion.

1870. God is said to permit evil for some greater good, which remains undefined.

1871. God is the grand metaphor
of who and what we are;
when we pray, we proudly say
we are the avatar
of wonderment afar.

1872. God must cherish the atheist, for his truth confronts eternal damnation.

1873. God's will determines what is right
while evil prowls both day and night.
If we do not help those in need,
we stand our ground and say "Godspeed."

1874. God would surely prefer those who do good because it is the right thing to do and not from fear of eternal damnation.

1875. God's moral imperative can be expressed in a single word: nonintervention.

1876. God-fearing virtue is a vice of sorts.

1877. If there is a God, he would prefer those who use their God-given intellect to question his existence.

1878. If we fail to protect an innocent child from evil, we are evil; and yet many worship an omnipotent God who allows immorality to prevail.

1879. Invoking God is intended to lend credence to what is said. The argument weakens with the creation of a deity.

1880. Our coins are inscribed "In God We Trust." Could we have done worse without this trust?

1881. Perhaps wandering black holes are an expression of God's displeasure with his creation.

1882. Some say God allows mass murder for the greater good. Such beliefs can only be said to embrace the absurd.

1883. The atheist honors God by using the intellect he has provided.

1884. The creation of God is an expression of existential despair.

1885. The incomprehensible prompts many to postulate the existence of a God.

1886. The notion of God is a search for meaning.

1887. The notion of God, however hazy, weaves its way to immortality in all who believe.

1888. The plethora of gods speaks to human need far more than truth.

1889. The trek from a first cause to a personal God is wrought with fear.

1890. Those who find fault with God acknowledge his existence. Perhaps they should reconsider.

1891. Those whom we have come to fear the most are the God-fearing.

1892. To believe we can entreat the creator of the universe for benefits is surely the sin of pride.

1893. Delivering one's son to death on the cross and allowing a flawed race to do its worst is a portrait of a loving God.

1894. To postulate a God to explain reality is to introduce the incomprehensible to make sense of the incomprehensible.

1895. To speak of God is to believe
what all of life denies.
Why not embrace with loving grace
a happy compromise?

1896. We ascribe unlimited powers to God without expecting commensurate responsibilities.

1897. We have proof of God's fallibility in the existence of humankind.

1898. When evil of the worst kind
      descends upon the race,
      God looks away, will not betray
      the rule to show no trace
      of his loving grace.

1899. Will God find those who do expect
      salvation as reward
      more worthy than those who suspect
      that virtue is untoward
      when done for room and board?

God and Guns

1900. God and guns are the dubious saviors of an
      immature race where God protects us from the
      horror of death and guns protect us from each
      other.

Golden Rule

1901. The Golden Rule thinks every fool has the same
      values.

Golf

1902. Putting a ball in a hole
      is difficult no doubt,
      but when it's more than a stroll
      seems a peculiar route.

Good Breeding

1903. Good breeding conceals any hint of superiority.

1904. Good breeding conceals the advantages that come from treating others well.

1905. Good breeding consists in disguising prejudice in pursuit of fair treatment and apparent harmony.

1906. Good breeding does not hold truth above harmony.

1907. Virtue without good breeding is indistinguishable from vice.

Good Fortune

1908. Good fortune expands one's bloodline endlessly.

Good Nature

1909. Good nature makes our shortcomings seem inconsequential.

Goodness

1910. Goodness is known to all who see;
no rule defines its way.
It spins a web of equity
known never to betray.

1911. Goodness is not defined by some God or religious position; it is simply a kind and loving heart.

1912. Those who say we are born good are blind to the self-serving world of childhood.

1913. Admonishing someone to be good for something fails to define "good" or "something." It opens the door to nearly any activity.

Goodwill

1914. Goodwill is best maintained by the use of generalities.

1915. Goodwill transcends good thought, for it strives for the welfare of all.

Gorilla

1916. The peaceful ape is often seen
as lower form of man;
seems we have much of the obscene
not found in this dark clan.

Gossip

1917. Gossip is evil in intent. Truth or falsehood is largely irrelevant.

1918. Gossip is merciless and is weakened only by ignorance.

1919. Gossip is rarely inspired by good deeds.

1920. Our love of gossip easily frees secrets from the confines of conscience, to the torment of all who dare to trust.

1921. The dark side of truth is not made noble by publication.

1922. Concealing truth can be a virtue.

1923. Spreading rumors of another's virtue would be a giant step forward in our evolution.

1924. When gossip inspires friendship, the human race can speak of progress.

Government

1925. A government practices child abuse when it labels a helpless infant illegitimate.

1926. A state that spies on its citizens and does not passionately protect privacy is unworthy of respect.

1927. Awards given by a flawed government may reveal recipients' shortcomings.

1928. Bad laws trivialize good ones.

1929. Capitalism serves the rich, whereas socialism makes sure there are no rich to serve.

1930. Considering the number of people who think clearly, the notion that law follows public opinion is unnerving.

1931. Government imbued with religious zeal is oppressive and warlike. The avowed morality of the righteous will not be denied.

1932. Governments do not respect the governed; they either fear or dominate them.

1933. Health care should not be subject to the bloody affair of capitalism.

1934. It is sad to note that many seek public office for private gain.

1935. Political electability is dependent on proposing simple solutions to complex problems.

1936. Powerful nations foster the full expression of our nature.

1937. Americans define their government and themselves by their unwillingness to vote.

1938. The conniving maneuvers of democracy's candidates for public office would be applauded by any despot.

1939. To be a good person, the good citizen must, at times, say no to government.

1940. The minority rules.

1941. The moral currency of the government we have come to know is clearly in default while it puts "In God We Trust" on its currency.

1942. The notion of one nation under God is offensive to those who think.

1943. The political leader committed to religion can easily slip into war in God's name.

1944. The vote: a thoughtless decision with monumental consequences.

1945. The vote is cast on wings of fancy, where style overwhelms substance.

1946. To assure the separation of church and state, those on the highest courts should be agnostics or atheists.

1947. When every tax is tied to income, there is little incentive to prosper.

1948. World interest, not national interest, is the key to human survival.

Grammar

1949. Sometimes it's best to ignore the rules and preserve the beauty of the line.

Gratitude

1950. Expectation of gratitude may find more than a trace of resentment.

1951. Gratitude is rarely able to compete with self-love.

1952. Gratitude should be found in the perfect memory of love.

1953. Those who give to elicit gratitude deserve none.

1954. To recall well gifts we bestowed
is pride that we best hide;
to forget loving gifts received
shows more of Mr. Hyde
than we dare confide.

Greatness

1955. Censure can be inspiring in pursuit of excellence.

1956. Exaggeration reveals the reverence we have for greatness.

1957. Failure in pursuit of excellence is not far from greatness.

1958. Greatness does not seek applause
and does what's right without laws.

1959. Greatness is an unbalanced pursuit of the singular.

1960. Greatness is diminished when we see it as the product of chance.

1961. Greatness is seldom assigned to those who provoke us with uncomfortable truth.

1962. Greatness must neglect much to succeed.

1963. Greatness reaches a high and low
the mediocre never know.

1964. Greatness sees with an inner eye
untouched by reason's lure.
It knows its way without delay;
'tis nature's cynosure.

1965. Greatness takes advantage.

1966. Greatness: some prevailed who should have failed.

1967. How many nobodies with greatness are consigned to circumstantial oblivion?

1968. Our criteria for greatness are as personal as our favorite color.

1969. Our need to worship ignores the dark side of those we call great.

1970. Some greatness can be heard by all,
like Daniels with a song.
Some shun the stage, will not engage,
as though they don't belong.
Seems Dickinson was wrong.

1971. The best known may not be the best.
Unknown greatness fails the test.

1972. The great are reluctant to share the prize.

1973. The great reveal the bias of fate.

1974. The greatness of the few is founded in the silence
of the many.

1975. The silent ones with greatness
who never look for fame
seem to me a royalty
deserving of a name—
pure goodness is their aim.

1976. The pedestrian is found in all great works. How
many poems of Dickinson do you recall?

1977. The pleasure some find in the faults of others
is surpassed only by the displeasure they find in
greatness.

1978. The truly great are found to be
excessive to the core;
no time for triviality
when thought seeks more and more
of what it must explore.

1979. The truly great see popularity as a setback.

1980. What unsuspected greatness there must be in the
few who choose anonymity.

1981. There is potential for greatness in those who do
not need to follow or to lead.

1982. Those we call great are mere favorites of chance.

1983. Those who see themselves as great have been misled.

1984. True greatness is rarely found
in those who lead the state.
With pride they find a battleground
to make their name with hate
while claiming all is fate.

1985. Wealth and position rarely bring one joy.
Those seen as great know power's dark employ.

Greed

1986. Greed, with its insatiable grasping for more and
more, is not far from poverty.

Grief

1987. Grief is confronted by an insipid stream of advice
found ever wanting.

1988. Grief's tearful language requires no translation.

1989. If our pains were seen by all,
envy would not make a call.

1990. Some grief is never old, for time stands still.

1991. The flow of time is said to take
grief to a kinder place,
but hearts have been known to break
with a last embrace.

1992. The grief that dissipates in time
was never born in love sublime.

1993. Those who grieve find love's encore,
phantom steps at the front door.

1994. When true love is lost, memory prevails.

Guest

1995. The face of a host is a fine timepiece.

1996. The ideal guest sends regrets.

Guilt

1997. A guilty soul can find no place
to hide from fear's tormented face.
The past is now the future's plight
and peace is ever out of sight.

1998. Freedom from guilt can be innocence of the worst
kind.

1999. Guilt defines our morality, but it may not curb
our behavior.

2000. Guilt is fear's home away from home, for there is
no place to hide.

2001. Guilt is genuine and profound when the
transgressions are beyond detection.

2002. Guilt is never worth the prize
for there is no compromise.
Peace comes only when one dies.

2003. Those who commit unspeakable crimes through
ignorance are still culpable.

2004. When deep regret inspires guilt,
the moral self is seen.
When evil reigns to the hilt,
some feel fine and clean—
shades of a human being.

Guns

2005. A gun in every hand is more than a reprimand.

2006. Gun elimination is the only effective gun control.

2007. Guns are dangerous because of who we are, not
what they are.

2008. If guns could be found apart from human beings,
we could argue they do not kill. Since guns and
people are inseparable, we must know guns do
kill.

2009. In a world where we stand our ground and guns
abound, there is no threat of overpopulation.

2010. It is not mental illness that causes thousands of
killings each year, but human nature.

2011. More guns will keep us safe, they say,
no other way to be:
time and again we pay to play
for eternity.

2012. Some say, "Keep guns away
from those who would do harm."
Faced with human nature,
whom would you disarm?

2013. The notion that societal safety is improved by
more guns in the hands of citizens is manifestly
absurd.

2014. Those who carry guns are inclined to use them.

2015. Destroying guns while allowing the gunmen to go
free accomplishes nothing.

2016. To disarm a population is to look human nature
squarely in the face.

2017. You can't outrun a gun.

Habits

2018. Constancy finds its way
to what we see as true;
we're easily led astray
by what we must pursue.

2019. Even beauty succumbs to the ritual of habit.

2020. Habit arising from need compels with the force of gravity. Escape velocity is rarely reached.

2021. Habit is the great normalizer.

2022. Habit is the habitat of thoughtlessness.

2023. Habit sees an unchanging world; it is thought's graveyard.

2024. Habit creeps its way to a place
where thought dare not show its face.
Some find a path that serves them well
while others submit to the spell
of rhythms—a mere bagatelle
of sights and sounds that compel.

2025. In a world in flux, the best of habits may need an update.

2026. Our bad habits are revealed to conceal our worst.

2027. The creation of good habits in youth is good fortune for a lifetime.

2028. The habit of writing has become a necessity that I welcome.

2029. The key to living well is to form habits deliberately and judiciously.

2030. The unpopularity of thought is seen in the plethora of habits.

Hair

2031. Gray hair reminds us of the inevitable.

Hands

2032. The hand is the appendage of speech and a telling measure of age.

2033. Those hands crippled by a lifetime of toil should bring shame to our race.

Happiness

2034. An ordinary day brings happiness to the wise.

2035. Few find happiness in the pursuit of truth.

2036. Fools find nothing satisfies their quest,
while wisdom sips the joy of love at rest.

2037. For happiness to endure, it must embrace the ephemeral.

2038. For me, the perfect happiness of any moment is diminished by the thought of being without my love.

2039. Goodness does not understand that evil can be happy.

2040. Grief must travel alone, but joy must *share* to be.

2041. Happiness can be found almost anywhere, for it is purely personal.

2042. Happiness does not appear to have any necessary connection to achievement or morality.

2043. Happiness endures the possibility of pain.

2044. Happiness is a funny thing,
can spring from any deed,
does not belong to right and wrong
but found in what we need.

2045. Happiness is as indefinable as the inscrutable human beings who claim its possession.

2046. Happiness is based on benign ignorance.

2047. Happiness is found in the fissures of our flawed nature; there is none in the world at large.

2048. Happiness is more likely to come from pursuit than from achievement.

2049. Happiness is most easily found in the lives of others.

2050. Happiness is nearsighted.

2051. Happiness is not prone to see
too clearly in the night;
it protects its sweet serenity
with blindness full of sight.

2052. Happiness is sometimes dependent on a soothing self-deception that one dare not challenge.

2053. Happiness sees rainbows without rain.

2054. Happiness that stems from the joy of others is rare indeed.

2055. Happy moments should be prized
with no thought of what will be,
for when we think, full of surmise,
we confront eternity—
far more joy in lovely lies.

2056. Health and love are the pillars of happiness.

2057. Humor can be a source of happiness even when its point is pain.

2058. If purpose is the crux of happiness, then anything goes.

2059. Ignorance is a reliable foundation of happiness.

2060. It is idealistic nonsense to suppose that character inevitably leads to happiness. One can be very good, very poor, and very miserable.

2061. Joy is varied, one must see.
There is no way to find the key
to certain bliss for you and me.

2062. Life is quite pointless without happiness.

2063. Looking forward to happiness places it forever out of reach.

2064. Sight puts happiness in jeopardy.

2065. Some are happy doing what is right;
some find dark deeds their delight.

2066. The closest many get to happiness is the hope that wealth is the answer.

2067. The happier we are, the more we have to lose.

2068. The happy have no need to convince others of their happiness.

2069. The happy love their fate;
'tis their ideal state.

2070. The kind are likely to be happy, but the happy can be cruel.

2071. The mathematics of joy favors division.

2072. The more we acquire, the more we desire in a futile pursuit of happiness.

2073. The more we strive to convince others of our happiness, the less it is so.

2074. The pursuit of happiness alone is ignoble, for it rarely is more than the gratification of desire.

2075. The pursuit of happiness inevitably fails. It is never a goal and always a consequence.

2076. There are few who have the wisdom to find happiness in wishes that come true.

2077. There is no greater happiness than an ordinary day with Joselita at my side.

2078. Those countries with the best history have the greatest happiness.

2079. Insidious comparisons make us wonder where we belong on the continuum of happiness.

2080. Those who are happy are blessed with the narrow vision of the satisfied.

2081. Those who have what we want may be miserable.

2082. Those who say happiness is the point of life preach an amoral doctrine.

2083. To compete for joy is to suppose
there is a place where we expose
life's highs and lows for all to see;
none has appeared in history.

2084. To find joy in another's win
is pure bliss without sin;
reveals a race well on its way
to goodness none betray.

2085. We like to think that happiness is imbued with morality, but the species with wisdom in its Latin name has found pleasure in the unforgivable.

2086. We pursue happiness without knowing what it means.

2087. We thrive on deprivation. Wanting something, however pointless, makes happiness possible.

2088. What makes us happy defines us.

2089. Writing thoughts that may not see the light of day
is my way of living life joyously.

Hardship

2090. Hardships are known to make us strong,
may lead us right or lead us wrong.
Perhaps it's best to judge a race
not by its strength but by its grace.

Harmony

2091. The best way to get along
with lovers and the rest
is to admit when we are wrong
and leave truth unaddressed.

2092. We creatively connect the dots and see harmony.

Haste

2093. Speed thrills, and speed kills; it is built into the
urgency of life.

2094. The habit of haste with its many missteps ensures
fast failure.

2095. The possible is reached in haste, but the probable
is the ally of deliberation.

Hatred

2096. Allowing hatred to dominate your life is a kind of suicide.

2097. Hate is inevitable and can be admirable.

2098. Hating yourself rather than hating others can be a first step to rehabilitation.

2099. One can hate evil with the emotional detachment of a logician.

2100. Profound evil demands hate.

2101. Love arising from hatred of a common enemy endures.

2102. To hate those we have injured is an admission of guilt.

2103. To hate those who hate us is simply immature.

2104. To never hate is to be amoral.

Head

2105. There is harmony between the head and the heart when we love what is good.

Health

2106. Health is seen when it disappears.

2107. I suspect that purpose enhances health with the effectiveness of a good deed and regular exercise.

2108. Occasional sickness brings appreciation of health, however fleeting.

2109. Perfect health is undetectable.

2110. Some do everything right and die early, whereas others break all the rules and live a hundred years. We do our best and leave the rest to fate.

2111. The doctrine of moderation in diet and exercise has not been improved upon in recent years.

2112. Those without health in childhood come to believe in fate.

2113. To put health care in the hands of private companies is to make wealth more important than health.

Heart

2114. A broken heart has done its best,
brought passion to each day.
The point of life to feel the zest
of striving, though we pay
with loss along the way.

2115. A broken heart has done more than try.

2116. A good heart adopts kindness as its first principle.

2117. The heart knows the answer before the question.

2118. The heart puts feeling and belief above reason.
In pursuit of truth, its triumphs are few, but its
conviction is sacrosanct.

2119. The heart that chooses symmetry over sense has
lost its way.

2120. Thought that consults the heart is more than
smart.

Heaven

2121. Heaven is seen when death is near,
hope's answer to pervasive fear,
a place where none would dare to say
no human being found this way.

2122. Heaven is the sweet lullaby
that lures when death is sure.
Our hopes find rest in a beau geste
for loss we can't endure.

Help

2123. Preaching is never confused with help.

Heredity

2124. All terrestrial life is written in the common language of DNA. We are special in our recognition that we are not so special.

Heroes

2125. As we approach a star, its beauty fades.

2126. Few heroes would remain so under scrutiny.

2127. Hero worship confuses the part with the whole.

2128. Heroism is difficult to define to the satisfaction of all. The willingness to die is crucial, but to die for what?

2129. Our heroes are rarely chosen for kindness.

2130. The gentle one who's truly kind
when all has gone awry
is heroism most refined
that brings a soulful sigh.

2131. There are heroic acts, but there are no heroes.

2132. Those wealthy individuals who do a few good deeds are treated as saints, while one who works twelve hours a day to support the family is ignored.

Hesitation

2133. Hesitation can save a life or cause a death; both chance and judgment play a role.

History

2134. A profound knowledge of history has not prevented war.

2135. History is a record of the conflict of ideals.

2136. Human history writes its message on the bloodstained landscape of ideologies.

2137. So long as self-interest dominates, our history has been written. The only path to survival is commitment to the well-being of the entire human race.

2138. To be a fan of the human race and be a historian would be remarkable indeed.

Holiness

2139. Holiness is a helpful place
where faith is said to reign.
What we believe serves to relive
the ever-present pain.

2140. The moment they speak of gods,
I think of those who play the odds.
They see the end so full of grief
and find sweet solace in belief.

Home

2141. The home is best that pulls us back
with love that's always there.
Though far away, we feel the sway
of those who truly care.

2142. To be good when away from home is the
beginning of morality.

Honesty

2143. Honesty can be an opinion, a weapon, a policy, a
slip of the tongue, or a mere statement of fact.

2144. Honesty is a state of mind where what we call
truth may be false and what we call lies may be
true.

2145. Honesty is not tolerated in polite company.

2146. Honesty with no compassion is cruelty justified.

2147. The straight lines of honesty do not allow the
curvature of compassion.

2148. Being true to yourself can bring disaster to millions.

2149. To confuse honesty with virtue is to confuse truth with goodness.

2150. Denying our very human nature can be a first step to virtue.

Honor

2151. Seems those who silently excel
are blessed by simply doing well.

Hope

2152. Hope battles reason and evidence in pursuit of happiness. One can only hope it will prevail.

2153. Hope becomes certainty when fear is great.

2154. Hope brightens a dark future with the light of unquenchable desire.

2155. Hope brings a full moon of possibilities that repel the dreadful night.

2156. Hope can be deception that sustains.

2157. Hope conquers all with flights of fanciful belief.

2158. Hope feeds on the improbable.

2159. When all has gone awry,
hope holds on tight with second sight
to dreams that will not die;
hope is our sweet ally.

2160. Hope is aware of terror in the night.

2161. Hope is full of creative denial. It is often useful
nonsense.

2162. Hope is full of heart and soul
untouched by reason's sight;
finds its way to faith's doorway
where the blinding light
of doctrine shows its might.

2163. Hope is inexhaustible wealth.

2164. Hope is often a delusion that sustains. It reveals
that the false can be superior to the true.

2165. Hope is sustained in a future just beyond our
grasp.

2166. Hope is the role future plays
in dreaming of what can be;
life is lost when hope overstays
with longings that don't see
what only love can be.

2167. Hope may be delusive, but it overcomes all
obstacles with effortless aplomb.

2168. Hope must remain finite to be believable.
Galaxies do collide.

2169. Hope overcomes fear with determined
self-deception.

2170. Hope puts truth in chains.

2171. Hope renounces the present in pursuit of some
insubstantial paradise.

2172. Hope shapes our world, creating a realm that
resonates with our deepest desires.

2173. Hope sustains us when we are confronted by cold
reason's pursuit of truth.

2174. Hope that finally comes to be
leaves only stark reality.
Our dreams make life seem much more
than daily chores with no encore.

2175. Hope validates fear.

2176. Hope's fear of pain is found in its ability to wish
for anything.

2177. It is better to strive for excellence than to hope for
recognition.

2178. Our youth fades quickly out of sight,
with hopes and dreams set free
to fade away in endless night
or find new ways to see.

2179. The darkest fear brings the brightest hope.

2180. The more we hope the world will be
a place where dreams come true,
the less we see reality
where no one has a clue.

2181. The suspension of critical thinking is hope's
greatest ally.

2182. We have no choice but to hope, considering the
alternatives.

Humanism

2183. Humanism is the rational alternative to theism.

2184. Those who choose to use their hands
to make a living fine
should not be seen as mindless bands
who must be kept in line.

Humanity

2185. A favor requiring recompense is debt in disguise.

2186. A society that needs a bible to be good is bound
to be bad.

2187. Among human beings, one's existence alone is
sufficient cause for being attacked. It is the nature
of the beast.

2188. Auschwitz fosters faith in man's depravity and God's indifference.

2189. Computers have been faithful servants in their infancy. Will the intelligent machines of tomorrow challenge Einstein and Shakespeare, or will they have an agenda more in keeping with humans' baser nature?

2190. Considering human potential, the pursuit of liberty is dangerous indeed.

2191. Criticism of others is one step away from self-discovery.

2192. Disappointment with humanity includes disappointment with ourselves.

2193. Driving in traffic in a large city reveals the flawed self-interest of our race. General welfare is rarely the goal.

2194. Each age sanctions its own madness in the name of propriety.

2195. God and guns serve those best who live in fear.

2196. A God who allows a world of pain
could be called inhumane,
while what we do and how we feel
oft reveals a heart of steel.

2197. History is known to repeat,
but we have found a way
with weaponry some say is sweet
to end it in a day.

2198. How quickly the extraordinary becomes ordinary with frequent exposure.

2199. Human nature makes no significant distinction between men and women.

2200. Humanity is a lesson in diminished expectations.

2201. Humanity, in every age, is an amalgam of ancestral types, from the primitive savage to the benign intellectual. Our behavior reveals that modernity is an illusion.

2202. "I must win" is the cry of the human race in its infancy.

2203. I sometimes dream my dad came back
to ask about the state of man,
looked in my face and knew the race
still killed and maimed for love of clan.

2204. If we create intelligent machines, we put all life in jeopardy, especially our own.

2205. Insofar as we value intelligence more than virtue, we are doomed.

2206. Intellect has many goals, but character strives only for the good.

2207. It is no surprise to find human beings with the sensitivity of the poet or the cold indifference of the serial killer.

2208. It is not our animality that brings shame, but an intellect that allows incomprehensible cruelty.

2209. It is sad to note that we could terraform Mars more easily than transform ourselves into a loving and peaceful species. Technical competence is unrelated to moral excellence.

2210. It is strange that declaring we are smart is offensive, but saying we have a good heart, which is far more significant, is acceptable.

2211. Humans are brilliant beasts, with poetry and pogroms in their repertoire.

2212. Many become poor in an effort to appear rich.

2213. Nature's motif is full of violence. The fact that we conceive of nonviolence is a step forward.

2214. Nothing is more ordinary than the wish to be extraordinary.

2215. Of all the natural forces that threaten our existence, none is more formidable than the human mind.

2216. One is not playing God when interfering in human affairs, for God does not intervene.

2217. Our aversion to peace suggests that the human race has just enough intelligence to bring about its own extinction.

2218. Our behavior on this planet conclusively shows that *Homo sapiens* have yet to appear.

2219. Our classification of life puts us at the pinnacle of creation. One wonders whether our unprecedented depravity is part of the evaluation.

2220. Our dark nature is exposed in the awful brilliance of the atomic age.

2221. Our flaws are magnified tenfold when found in others.

2222. Our human nature is a cluster of fears hidden from view by one pretense or another.

2223. Our species has repeatedly shown there is no need to postulate a supernatural source of evil.

2224. Our species has wisdom in its name but not in its heart.

2225. Our Stone Age heritage is revealed in a morality of don'ts.

2226. Our survival is dependent on the exercise of restraint, not the pursuit of liberty.

2227. Pursuit of wealth and love of war
can easily be found,
while doing good because we should
is simply felt unsound—
human nature unbound.

2228. Some long-term human relationships endure every indignity. They become necessary for survival.

2229. Terminal illness in others is often viewed as trivial compared to our own slight discomfort.

2230. The danger of intelligence is grimly revealed by a species that kills to honor its gods and relieve boredom.

2231. The dust blows, and we wonder who was there.

2232. The fact that we are aware of the inevitable is the tragedy of our species.

2233. The human race has improved killing machines to express a nature that remains unimproved.

2234. The indifference of a universe with wandering black holes puts self-importance in perspective.

2235. The many who do not think at all live in a shallow grave of pointless platitudes.

2236. The more we see of humanity, the less we see of sacrifice. Self-interest predominates.

2237. The potentiality for goodness is congenital; as we grow, we must decide.

2238. The unrealized potential for good is a source of profound disappointment with humanity.

2239. The warm and loving nature of humanity can easily be seen in the outliers among us.

2240. The word *humane* fails to describe the human race of my acquaintance.

2241. There is no better example of the incorrigible than a race that creates formidable weaponry and continues to wage war.

2242. To believe in the perfectibility of humans is to deny all evidence to the contrary. There is no sign that love and kindness will eventually emerge as the essence of who we are.

2243. To explain human behavior using Occam's razor is to grossly underestimate the subtle schemes of our species.

2244. To find pleasure in the pain of others is entirely human.

2245. To love all of humanity is to be amoral.

2246. To speak well of everyone is to speak well of no one.

2247. War and worship are the two failed strategies that dominate human behavior.

2248. We are fifty thousand years old when it comes to human nature and modern to the core when it comes to technology. We are Stone Age humans with the power to destroy the planet.

2249. We are hated for our strengths and loved for our flaws—so much for the perfectibility of man.

2250. We define a person's worth by schooling, employment, and wealth, while rarely looking at character.

2251. We have conceived of kindness and love, and we can only hope we evolve into truly moral beings.

2252. We have conclusively demonstrated that intelligence can put all life in jeopardy.

2253. We have ridden time's tumultuous steed through countless ages, only to find the hunter-gatherer within.

2254. We invoke heredity to excuse the inexcusable.

2255. We pray to gods and vote for candidates along party lines delivered to us by predecessors who did exactly the same.

2256. We program machines to run on logic while allowing ourselves the luxury of lunacy.

2257. We safely praise ourselves with the admission of error.

2258. We tend to look down on ordinary people, not realizing that most of us are unremarkable in most ways.

2259. We wrap ourselves in so many personas that there's no telling who we are.

2260. What omnipotent God would claim to be our father?

2261. What we perceive as opposition is merely self-interest.

2262. When a world leader proudly announces the killing of an adversary, however evil, he is defining our species.

2263. When we say, "That's human nature," we are rarely conferring a compliment.

2264. Although knowledge doubles every decade, *Homo sapiens* lack the wisdom to live in peace.

2265. Wildlife can be dangerous when hungry, but humans can kill when in the mood. To be human is to be feared.

2266. "You're not even human" is clearly a compliment.

Human Relations

2267. An extremely beautiful woman finds she can communicate with a man on only one subject.

2268. Better to ask for favors than insist on rights.

2269. Freedom of speech is reciprocal—beware!

2270. In human relations, it is better to be reflective than reactive.

2271. No one with insight wishes to appear natural.

2272. One must learn to ignore the opinions of inept people; they abound.

2273. Society demands we take charge or take orders. Is there no room for one who finds followership and leadership equally distasteful?

2274. Those who know us best admire us least.

2275. We create personas to satisfy a world that cares little for the person behind the mask.

2276. We often accept others when we change ourselves.

Humility

2277. Among civilized people, self-knowledge makes pride impossible and humility certain.

2278. Humility assumes a common set of values that may not exist.

2279. Humility is discreet self-praise.

2280. Humility is full of lies,
proudly weaving the right disguise.

2281. Humility is a mask for vanity more often than for greatness.

2282. Humility is pride made palatable.

2283. Humility may be no more than an insightfully honest assessment of oneself.

2284. Humility reveals one's belief in one's own superiority or the conviction that one is not worthy of special consideration. I believe our impact on our planet and each other reveals the truth of the latter sentiment.

2285. Humility wins respect by deception when silence would do.

2286. We do not seek humility, but if we learn life's lessons, it will find us.

Humor

2287. Best to find a way
to laugh at who we are.
Let humor have its say,
part of our repertoire.

2288. Humor trivializes whate'er it touches.

2289. Humor's superficial wit
prompts a woman to forget
where love and devotion sit.

2290. Finding pleasure in the pain of others reflects more a sense of meanness than a sense of humor.

2291. Those who say humor can assuage any tragedy feel nothing.

2292. We are all legitimate targets of humor. To take ourselves seriously is to be blind to our nature.

Hunting

2293. To truly oppose hunting is to be a vegetarian.

2294. When hunting is a sport, it is pure savagery, and one can only wish the predator would become the prey.

Hypocrisy

2295. A world that worships appearances encourages the hypocrisy it condemns.

2296. Hypocrisy may conceal virtue in pursuit of peer acceptance.

2297. Hypocrites who play their parts too well may buy that which they wish to sell.

2298. The hypocrite is sincerely insincere.

2299. Concealment of virtue is hypocrisy that we may find acceptable.

2300. Without hypocrisy, the razor-sharp tongue of truth would sever the warmest of relationships.

I

2301. "I" is an effective pronoun when revealing mistakes.

Ideals

2302. Ideals define what we wish to do and have not done; they define our shortcomings.

2303. Ideals flourish in the rarefied air of abstract thought, where the real is kept at bay.

Ideas

2304. A new and compelling idea may be a deathblow to what you must believe. You may need to decide between truth and personal well-being.

2305. A subject is closed to new thought once an idea is completely accepted.

2306. Brilliant ideas make experience unnecessary.

2307. Great ideas enrich life or reveal truth, and occasionally, they do both.

2308. In a changing world, ideas that do not keep pace will perish.

2309. Insight mysteriously arises as though it was always there.

2310. The brilliant insights that brought understanding of nuclear fission have brought more jeopardy than joy.

2311. The more we think, the less we are sure of anything.

2312. There are old ideas, such as peace on Earth, that would appear new and vital if they were finally implemented.

2313. When one is exposed to few ideas, there is real danger of being imprisoned by thought.

2314. When ideas abound, there is little chance of any one of them taking over our life.

Identity

2315. The keyhole's voice is found to be
the measure of identity.

2316. Thought wrestles with experience to make us who we are.

2317. We label everyone we greet
and think we know them well;
but deep inside we never meet
the one who will not tell.

Ideology

2318. Ideologies separate us into belief systems that rarely appeal to reason. Our needs and aspirations will not be confined by logic.

Idleness

2319. Better idleness than the energetic pursuit of evil.

2320. Busyness does not ensure virtue, nor does idleness necessarily lead to vice.

2321. Doing nothing at all is close to impossible. Those who engage in what we see as pointless pursuits are said to idle.

2322. Doing nothing may merely be recognition of the nothingness that is our fate.

2323. I have written several books with the understanding that in the scheme of things, my musings will vanish without a trace. The fate of idleness is the fate of all.

2324. Idleness is pure freedom.

2325. Idleness is the place to be
when wishing to create.
You may find your way to poetry
or simple sit and wait
for what is surely fate.

2326. If being idle brings you pain,
you have only yourself to blame,
for thought is free to find its way
to dreams and schemes above the fray.

2327. To never harm another living thing is an idleness difficult to disparage.

2328. To see idleness as evil is nonsense unworthy of refutation.

Idolatry

2329. Devotion to critical thought breaks idols in pursuit of truth.

2330. Worshiping virtue is without fault.

2331. We worship those with wealth unbound,
their names known to us all.
The thoughtful few we never knew
consigned to be so small—
one wonders why they call.

If

2332. Those terrifying *ifs* that paralyze with possibilities make fear our reality.

If Only

2333. "If only" is softly spoken
in thoughts of might-have-been.
No harm in heartfelt tokens,
in reveries that pretend.

2334. "If only" is the sad refrain
of all who face life's harsh terrain.
Better to see the many ways
life has brought joy and lovely days.

2335. The present is all we have;
all else is in the mind.
"If only" is the cry of those
who lose their life in time.

Ignorance

2336. Acknowledge ignorance and wonder.

2337. Deep study stumbles upon the abyss of ignorance.

2338. Ignorance can bring peace when knowing changes nothing.

2339. Ignorance is foundational.

2340. Ignorance is proud of what it knows.

2341. Ignorance is revealed in conviction.

2342. Ignorance keeps us alive with inquiry.

2343. Ignorance of ignorance
is the easy way to show
you believe without question
what you do not know.

2344. Not knowing what is always done and what is thought impossible is advantageous ignorance.

2345. The more fundamental the question, the greater
the ignorance.

2346. The quest for ignorance is satisfied in implacable
belief.

2347. Awareness of ignorance is a kind of knowledge.

2348. We find that knowing can bring pain
while ignorance is sweet gain.
The world is such a troubled place,
seems good and bad can't keep pace.

2349. What we do not understand should prompt
inquiry, not fear or adoration.

2350. What we know is the coastline of the vast
continent of ignorance.

2351. Who can quarrel with ignorance that fosters a
happy life?

Illness

2352. Some few may come when we are old
with grief put on for show.
There may be one where tears enfold,
where love knows only woe.

2353. The ills that do not come our way
should be a source of joy today,
for oft the ills we're forced to bear
are less than those that bring despair.

2354. The relief of severe physical pain becomes a goal more important than our survival. All other ills vanish in the presence of profound pain.

Illusion

2355. As we age, life's lessons make it increasingly difficult to sustain our illusions. Clear vision may bring more sorrow than joy.

2356. Illusions are what most live by,
sustain us every day.
When truth destroys a cherished lie,
our life has lost its way.

2357. Attacking a life-sustaining illusion is not far from attempted murder.

Imagination

2358. Fictional characters populate our lives, and the real ones only occasionally reveal their sway.

2359. Imagination that is productive finds reason in hot pursuit.

2360. Reason sees death's door, but imagination overcomes with possibility.

2361. The greater our experience and therefore our years, the more imagination can play its part, pursuing its art.

2362. When we escape the present into what might have been or what might be, we use our intelligence in the time travels of thought.

Imitation

2363. Even our thoughts are often plucked from those favored by our culture and prized by followers who abound.

2364. Freedom favors imitation.

2365. Imitation appears easier than thought until we look in the mirror.

2366. Imitation is the sincerest form of inadequacy.

2367. Self-respect knows little of imitation.

2368. The thing imitated is often the result of imitation.

2369. There is no need to imitate
the evil that is seen,
for such deeds darkly innate
seem part of some foul gene.

2370. We imitate because we find
something we see as great.
'Tis love that molds our state of mind
with what we would create
blessed with a kinder fate.

Immigration

2371. Is entering a country illegally equivalent to breaking into one's own home?

Immortality

2372. Fear and desire create an immortal soul that belief sustains without a scintilla of evidence.

2373. For me, the only immortality of merit is the love of one human being for another.

2374. If immortality means repeating life's cycles ad infinitum, many would opt out.

2375. Immortality is a symbol without a referent; nothing endures.

2376. Many yearn for immortality to engage in trivial pursuits untouched by the meaningful.

2377. Science is replete with jeopardy when it comes to what we know of existence. Endless cycles of birth and death are all we can see on the horizon.

2378. Some who yearn for immortality find an eternity of golf and bridge irresistible.

2379. The desire for immortality is conditional.

2380. Denying the possibility of immortality is, for many, unforgivable.

2381. To embrace immortality, one must reject all rational thought and experience. Oblivion is nature's answer to existence.

2382. A return to the fiery cauldrons of the cosmos is an immortality unworthy of the name.

2383. Those who say we must be immortal have found their path to peace. Let compassion set aside your passion for truth.

2384. Those who speak of immortality know nothing of cosmology.

2385. Without love, immortality is a nightmare without end.

Impatience

2386. Impatience expects problems to have easy solutions. Those who are impatient are angry with a world that fails to bend to their will.

Impossibility

2387. Impossibilities are easy to recognize when we lack the will to persist.

2388. In a world where existence is the fundamental mystery, the word *impossible* should be used sparingly.

Impression

2389. In making a good impression, humility rarely fails. One's honest opinion or actual truth is not likely to be well-received.

2390. There is little point in trying to make an impression, for what we *are* speaks volumes.

Improvement

2391. Improvement brings satisfaction contingent upon ignoring our fate.

2392. When we find joy in the welfare of others, we will have improved.

Impulse

2393. Rationalization wraps our impulses in the attire of what must be.

2394. Those who decry the expression of primeval impulses have looked deeply into our very human nature.

2395. War is surely an expression of primeval impulses that, on the battlefield, are given full reign.

Inactivity

2396. Taking the long view, to see our inactivity as a flaw is to give ourselves too much importance.

Income

2397. Income should be limited by government to avoid the tyranny of great wealth and to bring welfare to all the citizens of the state.

Incomprehensible

2398. The incomprehensible begins with existence.

Inconsistency

2399. Inconsistency defines the thoughtful.

2400. Inconsistency reveals rough edges of creative thought. Straight lines are nowhere to be found.

Indecision

2401. A plethora of thought bars the drive to action.

2402. Ignorance is the best reason for indecision.

2403. Indecision may be, in the end, the inability to distinguish between good and evil.

Independence

2404. To be independent of one's culture in any substantive way is to be thought dangerous indeed.

2405. Refusal to kill is an expression of independence maligned by most "civilized" societies.

2406. We are nurtured by culture, which makes independence of thought more than rare.

2407. We wish to value above all
the nonconforming soul;
we end up with the protocol
that safely plays a role.

Index

2408. A writer's thoughts are lost in a vast wilderness without some sort of index.

Indifference

2409. Indifference is nature's ally.

2410. Indifference seems so cruel, and then we reflect on God.

Indiscretion

2411. Indiscretion treats friends and foes alike; it extends cruelty to include all.

2412. The indiscreet do not hate;
they merely capitulate.

Individuality

2413. Individuality proudly proclaims its freedom, while remaining subject to the tyrannical twins, nature and nurture..

2414. Nature and nurture contrive to make us one of a kind, and yet we strive to be one of the many.

2415. Our classifications of life dispose of individuality with indifferent arrogance.

2416. The individualist refuses to be the specialist who is oblivious to the matrix of meaning that defines our existence.

2417. The individualist refuses to succumb to a society that insists on blending the elements of our diverse nature into a unified conformity of thought and action.

2418. The monsters among us reveal the dark side of individuality.

2419. To praise individuality without qualification is to ignore the human nature we have come to know.

2420. We prefer comfortable copies to outrageous originals.

2421. We speak of the individual while we deal with stereotypes.

Indolence

2422. Contemplation of our fate fosters thoughtful laziness.

2423. How many with potential greatness have decided not to pursue what will inevitably disappear?

Indulgence

2424. Consequences are rarely seen
when hunger must be fed;
our thoughts lie somewhere in between
our stomach and our head.

Inevitable

2425. The inevitability that always comes to mind is the loss of loved ones; those of us who love are torn apart by life.

2426. Those who advise us to ignore the inevitable say we should be content while being fully aware of impending disaster.

Infancy

2427. Infants conform to nature's programming while we respond to their every whim.

Infidelity

2428. Infidelity is a virtue when promises are made to evil.

Influences

2429. The desire to be accepted is rarely an influence that endures or makes us proud.

2430. When we are influenced by the famous nobodies who abound, we have found our place in the scheme of things.

Information

2431. Information may have little to do with meaning.

Ingratitude

2432. Ingratitude seems appropriate when one experiences profound infirmity.

2433. Ingratitude sees good fortune as an entitlement.

Inheritance

2434. The weeping heir finds solace in death.

2435. Those who share an inheritance are more than acquaintances.

Injury

2436. Injurious words are best met
with no response and no regret.

2437. The injuries we do to others are often thought
justified, but those we suffer wild-eyed..

2438. To have injured another
is to see the tortured face
of a self who will never
forgive the one debased.

2439. Ignoring an injury encourages its repetition.

Innocence

2440. Innocence has more to do with finding evil
inconceivable than with being ignorant of its
existence.

2441. Innocence sees nothing sinister.

2442. The innocence of childhood is rarely seen in the
sharing of toys.

2443. The innocent cannot know
the beauty of their state,
for knowledge casts a shadow
we cannot escape.

2444. Being without shame is not the same as virtue.

Inquiry

2445. The more fervent the belief, the less tolerance for
inquiry.

Insensibility

2446. Being indifferent to another's pain
is true of many who claim to be humane.
Words find their way to portraits that reveal
the face of one whose heart is made of steel.

Insight

2447. Insight that makes experience unnecessary is rare
indeed.

2448. Insights that arise from tragedy make us long for
ignorance.

Insomnia

2449. Insomnia can be a blessing when one awakens at three o'clock in the morning to a new poem.

Instinct

2450. Animal instinct promotes survival, whereas human intelligence has contributed to the deaths of millions.

2451. Those who encourage us to follow our instincts should note that the monsters among us have done exactly that.

2452. What instinct knows, reason explains.

Institutions

2453. Institutions dominate every society, and our survival is tied to adaptation.

Insult

2454. To respond to an insult is to give it weight.

Insurance

2455. Insurance: an investment in fate.

Integrity

2456. Integrity should not be confused with virtue, for one can honestly proclaim evil intent.

2457. Success, even more than failure, threatens integrity.

2458. Those who make their living writing or speaking are careful not to be too thoughtful, lest they lower their income.

Intellectual

2459. An intellectual is not confined by the certainties of the day.

2460. An intellectual is one who passionately pursues knowledge, while never allowing passion to sway judgment.

Intelligence

2461. A powerful intellect can conceive of many things that simply do not exist.

2462. A powerful primate brain magnifies both pleasure and pain.

2463. All this talk of humans' future godlike intelligence fails to mention the human nature we've come to know.

2464. Brilliance and belief in a personal God reveal the variable nature of intelligence in any individual.

2465. Brilliance in one subject is no guarantee of brilliance in another. Intelligence is in a state of flux.

2466. Confronted with the counterintuitive leaps of quantum mechanics, we can all complain about our intelligence, for conclusions are tentative and full of doubt.

2467. How would we appear to superior alien visitors? Perhaps they would see us as we see the chimpanzee, or because of our killing on a grand scale, they may put us in another category.

2468. Intelligence brings jeopardy unknown to the dull.

2469. Intelligence has proved to be a dangerous attribute, for it has allowed us to prevail.

2470. Intelligence has proved to be
the scourge of humanity.
We find more ways to kill our kind,
then all we see with little mind.

2471. Intelligence is applauded
no matter what its course,

while doing good or what we should
is sadly without force.

2472. Intelligence is costly, for it dismisses the untenable
beliefs that sustain millions.

2473. Intelligence is deadly without wisdom.

2474. Intelligence is easily corrupted by fear and desire.

2475. Intelligence is the ability to solve a problem, to
reach a goal. It is essentially amoral.

2476. Intelligence provides humans the potential to be
much better than the other animals. It is sad to
note that few have chosen the selfless pursuit of
virtue.

2477. Intelligence sees an advantage in stupidity.

2478. The term *intelligence*, like any symbol outside of
mathematics, fails to capture the dynamic reality
to which it refers.

2479. Nature selected intelligence to survive and prevail,
putting all life in jeopardy.

2480. No known species has yet appeared that can be
trusted with high intelligence.

2481. One would expect to find a cerebral manifestation
of a fine memory, but genius is far too subtle to
reveal its source.

2482. The more intelligent accept being called stupid,
for they know they have been stupid so often.

2483. There are times when silence reveals intelligence.

2484. There is no greater threat to human survival than human intelligence.

2485. Creating machines smarter than we are smacks more of ego than intelligence.

2486. To develop machines with intelligence is to ignore our example.

2487. Speaking well of our intellect is the ultimate faux pas, but speaking of our good heart is hardly noticed. Apparently, saying you're smart is bragging, but saying you're good is irrelevant.

2488. Two empty heads are not better than one.

2489. We have shown that greater intelligence does not inevitably lead to a reverence for life.

Intelligent Design

2490. Intelligent design is no more than the will to believe. It postulates, a priori, the existence of a supreme creator who confers eternal life. It is an abortive attempt to cloak religion with the semblance of science.

2491. The human body, which is the intelligent designer's consummate achievement, is replete with flaws that may be corrected by the clumsy trial and error of evolution.

Intention

2492. Intentions are best kept in silence.

2493. Intentions wrapped in words are rarely opened.

Introspection

2494. Honest introspection cannot coexist with conceit.

Intuition

2495. Intuition knows nothing of process.

2496. Intuition transcends schooling with insight untouched by rules of reason.

Invention

2497. Invention should not be confused with improvement. It is our nature to invent and have our own way.

2498. Inventions multiply our needs endlessly.

Irony

2499. Irony brings a deeper truth.

2500. Irony, with subtlety and sting, censures with seeming praise.

Irreplaceable

2501. There is one who has come to be
my north, south, east, and west;
were she to go, humanity
would fail every test.

Irresolution

2502. Irresolution is good when intentions are bad.

Jealousy

2503. Jealousy is admission of perceived inferiority.

2504. Jealousy rejects the pervasive impact of chance on every aspect of our lives. The jealous cannot accept not being the favorite of fortune.

2505. Love without jealousy should go by some other name.

2506. Those who do their best and leave the rest to fate have no time for jealousy.

Jeopardy

2507. The magma of Yellowstone reminds us that we are all on the hot seat.

Journalism

2508. A free press, wrapped in Jeffersonian virtue, pursues its own interests in the name of public welfare.

2509. The freedom of the press includes the freedom to destroy lives.

2510. Great journalists engage in deliberation before publication.

2511. The journalist who befriends those in power should leave the profession.

Joy

2512. Conceal joy and be kind
    to many who know pain.
    Better we appear blind
    when sight is inhumane.

2513. grief needs no companion, while joy's life expectancy is brief when alone.

2514. Joy is the precious heartbeat
of one who's at my side;
no other treat is half so sweet
as love bona fide.

2515. Life has so many, many ways
of bringing wondrous mirth;
for me, joy rests in the clichés
of lovers round the Earth.

2516. Moments of great joy are heights that prompt
some to see the inevitable darkness below.

2517. One must share a joy or let it go;
it takes two beneath the mistletoe.

2518. Our greatest joys are found in this:
a quiet life and good-night kiss.

2519. To spend life seeking moments of rapture is to
lose those many ordinary days we would give
anything to retrieve.

Judgment

2520. Fluency in a dozen languages cannot compare to
knowing when to be silent in one.

2521. Good judgment is bad judgment revisited.

2522. Judgments always reflect sincere bias.

2523. Our flawed judgments pursue us throughout life,
and yet we are reluctant to acknowledge them.

2524. Refusal to judge is a kind of judgment.

2525. We think for ourselves within the confines of culture. We are never alone in our judgments.

Justice

2526. Clever lawyers put us all in jeopardy.

2527. In the name of justice, prisons welcome the poor, and courts court the rich.

2528. Jurors can effectively challenge bad laws if they vote their conscience.

2529. Our sense of justice is tied to the constitution of our thought.

2530. The human race would do better in a court of injustice where a defense is possible.

2531. The judge who insists that jurors follow a law even when that law violates their conscience is in the service of tyranny.

2532. Those who say God is just must see the evil that abounds as part of his justice.

2533. To seek justice is to seek pain, for no one reaches moral perfection.

Kindness

2534. Acts of kindness tend to unite us if the underlying motives are not examined too carefully.

2535. Even kindness is suspect when extended to one who we know will continue to do harm.

2536. If we need to cultivate kindness, it may be more device than virtue.

2537. It is difficult to object to kindness, no matter what its source.

2538. Kindness is the jewel of memory, outlasting all the wit and wealth you can find.

2539. Kindness given with no thought of gain soars far above all heavens we attain.

2540. Kindness is more than a state of mind.

2541. Kindness is unpaid debt.

2542. Nice guys finish first in every contest that matters.

2543. One would think that kindness would be far more popular than it appears to be, for it is known to help those who give more than those who receive.

2544. The act of returning a kindness should not be confused with the real thing.

2545. Some truth is full of treachery,
      its only purpose pain;
      some lies are full of sympathy,
      the way to be humane—
      true lies in love's domain.

2546. The source of truly great kindness, we will never
      see, for it insists on anonymity.

2547. True kindness is empathy that feels the jeopardy
      that can touch us all.

Kiss

2548. A kiss is elusive,
      for it's never the same;
      it may be pleading
      or passion aflame.
      No matter its purpose,
      it can be sublime,
      for where in this world
      are such moments in time?

Knowledge

2549. Acquired knowledge brings comfort to
      mediocrity.

2550. Agnosticism serves knowledge by its admission of
      ignorance.

2551. All of our knowledge rests upon the fundamental mystery of existence.

2552. Awareness of ignorance is knowledge we can rely on.

2553. Certainty is found in the perfect knowledge of fools.

2554. Doctoral ignorance is preserved in the dogma of degrees.

2555. Experience wraps knowledge in the real, seeing pitfalls that only living can provide.

2556. Ignorance can bring joy unknown to knowledge.

2557. Insight sheds its own light.

2558. It is what we presume to know that puts us in danger.

2559. Knowledge is valid insofar as it recognizes its limitations. All that we know rests on a vast reservoir of ignorance.

2560. Knowledge should rest on possibilities, which rarely harden into belief.

2561. Our minds rose from the mire
with sight not seen before.
To know has been a curse,
for it sees nevermore.

2562. Our world cannot be the world, for perception is a creative process.

2563. Perception confines the world to our biology.

2564. Profound knowledge of an occupation reveals its dark side. A perfect job is perfect nonsense.

2565. Seeing many sides of an issue often ends in that state of knowledge called confusion.

2566. The more we think we know, the less we are likely to find out. Questioning what is accepted as true rarely fails to inform.

2567. The refined weaponry of the twenty-first century serve to refute the Socratic notion that knowledge is virtue.

2568. Deducing empirical facts without direct experience is knowledge of the deepest kind.

2569. Knowing nothing about something brings the comfort of certainty.

2570. Knowing what you don't know is the only perfect knowledge.

2571. To see ignorance where our knowledge is most profound is to know.

2572. We dress events in thoughts that we take for reality.

2573. We think we know the time when we have only one watch.

2574. What is thought to be known can be the greatest obstacle to future discovery.

2575. What we do not want to know comes close to untested belief.

2576. When knowing brings pain, let ignorance reign.

2577. When writing a book of aphorisms, one is plagued by the thought that the offerings are trivial and already known.

Labor

2578. The pleasure in writing is balanced by the irksome attention to detail required by the book.

2579. Labor has found a new ally
that never fails to persevere.
Machines work hard and never die,
are born to one career—
no humans need appear.

Language

2580. Competence in several languages does not lead to mastery of one.

2581. Expletives communicate with a clarity rarely found where propriety is the order of the day.

2582. Good or bad: a world of polar opposites is more in tune with language than with reality.

2583. It is difficult to escape the world defined by our native language.

2584. There are times when concealing knowledge is a virtue.

2585. When abstract thought finds its home in the particular, it creates language that speaks to us all.

2586. When language both informs and feels, it defines us and our world.

2587. Words wind round every experience, confining *the* world to the stereotypes of our time and place.

Laughter

2588. A hearty laugh can reveal
a kind soul or heartless heel.

2589. If laughter prevents tears, the suffering must be slight.

2590. Laughter can come from any place,
depending on who we are.
It may bring joy to the human race,
leaving an awful scar.

2591. Laughter found to be unkind
reveals malice well-defined.

2592. Laughter has the integrity of the confessional.

2593. Our laughter reveals who we are,
no matter what we say.
It's deeper far than a memoir,
for thought cannot betray
a loud laugh's vérité.

2594. To laugh at oneself is to confirm the opinions of
others.

2595. When we laugh at ourselves, we reveal both
courage and character.

Law

2596. A right to bear arms has been expressed as a right
to kill.

2597. All law should by its very nature reward virtue.

2598. An adversarial system focused on winning has
nothing to do with truth or justice.

2599. Law may for a time change our behavior, but not
our nature.

2600. Law never follows the example of God, for it
chooses to intervene.

2601. Laws are tyrannical when they favor the few.

2602. Laws evolve in times of war.

2603. Laws that force us to fight are fully consistent
with the cruelty of nature.

2604. Perfect adherence to law is bound to be wrong in a world where government is imperfect.

2605. Reason creates law that is inevitably modified by experience.

2606. Some laws should be immutable; the killing of innocents should never be condoned.

2607. The law may define a right that is dead wrong.

2608. The law of God embraces everything that is.

2609. The more laws, the less justice, for special interests multiply, and general welfare is lost.

2610. The strength of the law derives from the penalty for transgression, but its morality may be no more than the sentiment of the day.

2611. Wealth and law find a way
to save face while they betray.

Leadership

2612. The impulse to follow is the foundation of leadership.

Learning

2613. Error teaches while example is ignored.

2614. Learning is what genius finds unsatisfactory.

2615. The learning we respect the most leads to wealth, not to wisdom.

2616. To see value in learning that we would rather reject is to become a student.

2617. We should be thankful for life's bad examples, for they have taught us well.

2618. We would learn more if we were willing to include the teachers we despise.

Leisure

2619. Aimlessness and dedication to some worthy goal end in the same place.

2620. For me, leisure has been a time to think and write.

2621. Hardships force us to learn, and leisure allows us to create.

2622. If you can sit and wonder, you have a degree of freedom unknown to those in pursuit of wealth and fame.

2623. Leisure can be a powerful catalyst for creative endeavor.

2624. Leisure with a philosophic bent never bores.

2625. Our leisure time defines us.

2626. The best educated find the leisure of retirement a delight.

2627. Those who are not prepared for leisure are not prepared for responsibility.

2628. To pursue leisure, untouched by the demands of achievement, is to appreciate the fragility and brevity of life.

Letters

2629. My books are letters written to the world.

Liberty

2630. Liberty finds in our very human nature an opportunity to do wrong on a grand scale.

2631. Liberty is a cage lined with laws.

2632. Liberty is bathed in the blood of a hundred armies, all driven by God-given rights.

2633. Only the most civilized among us are not betrayed by liberty.

2634. Religious liberty is the right to believe the improbable in pursuit of eternal life.

2635. The liberty to bear arms has made the United States the killing capital of the world.

2636. The liberty to follow one's conscience can lead to killings galore.

2637. Until self-control is part of our profile, liberty is dangerous indeed.

2638. When liberty goes awry, we yearn for the tyranny of order.

Lies

2639. A lie that spares one pain
is censured by the few
who see the mark of Cain
in anything untrue.

2640. A lie with a tincture of truth
endures with the power of proof.

2641. Considering the thoughts that cross our minds,
locks in the form of lies seem prudent.

2642. For many, lies are the sustaining pillars of life.

2643. Honest lies are truths designed to deceive.

2644. Lies are found to coat the truth with doubt.

2645. Lies sustain us, for the truth may be without compassion.

2646. To chase a lie, we make it grow,
and truth is lost in a sideshow.

2647. To never tell a lie is cruelty refined.

Life

2648. A life full of discord is easier to lose, whereas a happy life finds the prospect of loss an ever-present fear.

2649. A time will come when hope is gone,
when all we have is what we've done.
We know the Earth so full of birth
will fill new hearts with longing spun
of faith and dreams that overcome.

2650. After eighty, I resist the impulse to dwell on the past by working on my next book.

2651. Care brings us closer to the end
while joy never fails to extend.

2652. Cosmology strongly suggests that human life will vanish without a trace.

2653. Desire is drenched in life; it sustains our every breath.

2654. Every moment of healthy life is precious, considering the eternity that awaits us.

2655. For me, love is the only reality that makes it all worthwhile.

2656. I disagree with those who say it doesn't matter how long we live, but how well. Old age gives a perspective denied to those who supposedly put much into a few years.

2657. If evolutionary paths randomly lead to intelligence, our example is a warning.

2658. If we were to live again, would we avoid life's pitfalls, or would our human nature be confronted with imperatives too powerful to ignore?

2659. In the mathematics of life, counting one's blessings comes first.

2660. It is presumptuous to say that life without any obvious achievement or zest is of no consequence. Watching the world go by is a source of wonder enough.

2661. Life is an introduction to death.

2662. Life is so full of life and death,
seems nothing's here to stay.
Hope lingers on our final breath
and finds a way to pray.

2663. Life is the joy of love and discovery, the torment of loss, and the pervasive presence of the ordinary.

2664. Life may be an anomaly of no consequence, but when we are alive, it is everything.

2665. Life's greatest blessing is love—hands down.

2666. Mathematics of life: the shortest distance between two points is defined by the unpredictable.

2667. No proof that life is precious can withstand our résumé.

2668. One can love deeply and pursue truth without embracing the fiction of immortality. Belief in the unbelievable is not needed to cherish every moment of life.

2669. Our tears flow over all we create, for nothing endures.

2670. Reverence for life has its limits.

2671. Straight lines are the shortest paths in Euclidean geometry, but life requires twists and turns to prevail.

2672. The brevity of the flower's bloom is life's eternal curse.

2673. The improbability of life makes anything seem possible.

2674. The inevitable nothingness does not dissuade us from embracing life as though it were eternal.

2675. The mystery of existence is brought to life by life.

2676. The second edition of my life, if permitted, would be edited extensively.

2677. There are times in every life when nonexistence seems preferable.

2678. Those who condemn a useless life rarely define "useful."

2679. Those who say time heals the profound wounds of life have never loved.

2680. To be free of folly is to never live.

2681. The suggestion to live intensely and die early is prescribed by the thoughtless.

2682. To recognize that a life is important is not to say that it is worthy.

2683. We confuse our nature with nature when we attempt to confine life to symbols.

2684. We live and wonder why we're here,
     imagine gods and more.
     We live awhile and disappear—
     a moment's metaphor.

2685. We seem to be no more than a remarkable product of evolution.

2686. Without our input, life has no purpose.

2687. We are reluctant to accept our membership in the world of animals without the expectation of eternal life.

2688. We hold on to some things and let go of others and define our lives.

2689. We take part in life when we're young, and we take life apart when we're old.

2690. When life goes wrong, we yearn for an ordinary day with its plethora of problems.

2691. When young, the poets spoke to me
with verse that touched my heart.
Life came along so full of song
I felt the source of art
in living every part.

Life and Death

2692. All of life is born in pain,
each mother will attest;
all of life will die in vain
when love is put to rest.

2693. Once tasting life, I cannot find
a way to welcome death.
Some plan for immortality
beyond our final breath—
religion's shibboleth.

2694. The dead are gone, but we hold on
to memories most dear,
as though to say on some fine day
they will reappear.
Hope—nothing but sincere.

2695. The flaws of those who die
wrapped in a kindly lie—
best way to say good-bye.

2696. The loss of love is the loss of life.

2697. The timeless rush of daily chores puts life and
death on hold.

2698. When worldly longings vanish, life and death are indistinguishable.

Like

2699. None are so blind who love their kind when all the world knows better.

Limits

2700. Aphorisms thrive on limits: the fewest words with the most thought.

2701. Four lines of verse can capture a world.

2702. Limits are barriers to be challenged; the struggle is the joy.

Literature

2703. It is literature when we are compelled to quote.

2704. Literature is found in memorable lines that enlighten experience.

2705. Literature imbues language with vitality, creating a living alliance of words and meaning.

2706. Literature leaps on the moment
in pursuit of all time,
seeks to capture life's vitality
in the eternal line.

2707. Literature may speak of life
while perched aloof, above the strife.

Logic

2708. A rigorous application of logic makes us
comfortable with the world inside our head.

2709. Flawless logic is more likely to persuade machines
than men.

2710. The purely logical mind untouched by flights of
fancy is no more than a machine.

Loneliness

2711. An abortive attempt to assuage loneliness can be
seen in the accumulation of more and
more possessions.

2712. Loneliness is overcome only by love's chains of
belonging.

2713. None are so lonely as those who've lost
the one whose life is dear.
All that remains is permafrost;
there's nothing left to fear.

2714. Silence is shattered by the lonely souls among us,
with words cascading in a cry for company.

2715. When we think of loneliness, love's spats are
warmly cherished.

Longevity

2716. One thousand years of work would surely test the
value of longevity.

Loss

2717. Absence is the saddest word
in a world where love is true;
searing silence can be heard
when one heart beats for two.

2718. Called an old friend to say hello
and received a strange reply.
He spoke as though he did not know
a staunch and dear ally,
lost in the mind's eye.

2719. Dear friends are gone forever now.
I remember them so well.
No day goes by without a sigh
for loss I can't dispel.

2720. Loss of a job can be the ultimate tragedy, for
one has no job to draw attention away from
misfortune.

2721. Lost love: the collapsing world closes every
door that once held promise, leaving only the
emptiness within.

2722. The hope we hold deep in our heart
remains through thick and thin;
we may have lost our counterpart,
but love will not give in.

2723. The loss of a loved one reveals life's meaning with
the poignant clarity of a teardrop.

2724. There are times that remind us all
of cycles that must be.
The death of one who once stood tall
brings tears for all to see.
Loss is our destiny.

2725. There is loss beyond the salve of friendship.

2726. We reach for past joy
and find it drenched in tears,
for memory only brings
the pain of lost years.

2727. When we sadly live to see
true love face eternity,
we wonder why we cherish birth
when all beauty turns to earth.

2728. Wisdom chooses ignorance
when knowing brings great pain;
I look away from that sad day
when fate may find her name
and nothing will sustain.

Love

2729. As years go by, our precious health
     competes with love and wondrous wealth,
     but in the end those by our side
     keep life alive before they die.

2730. Belief in love makes life worthwhile,
     all other ways no more than guile.
     The love I feel when she walks by
     inspires all to softly sigh.

2731. "Blood is thicker than water" is only for those
     who have never loved. Love transcends all blood
     boundaries.

2732. Caution in love is a contradiction.

2733. Does the freedom cherished by the gurus of love
     include infidelity?

2734. Even love is suspect, for one can love to inflict
     pain.

2735. Evil can be cherished in the name of unqualified
     love.

2736. For many, the choice of a mate is a matter more
     of need than of worth.

2737. For me love is the greater part
     of life's brief here and now,
     for only matters of the heart
     give meanings that endow
     with lasting joy somehow.

2738. Heartstrings make puppets of us all.

2739. Her beauty shed a wondrous light
that brought us to our knees;
enchanted by the stunning sight,
we reel in reveries
of love's haunting tease.

2740. How can one love and welcome death?

2741. Humanity's greatest achievement is love and the art that celebrates it.

2742. Hyperbole is the natural language of love.

2743. If love is involuntary, then fidelity is never secure.

2744. If we love our enemies and our enemies are evil, then we embrace evil and dishonor love.

2745. If wisdom is accepting the world as it is, then no one who loves can ever be wise.

2746. If you love your enemy who is profoundly evil, do you love evil?

2747. In modern romance, one sees a succession of pairings, driven by "never be alone."

2748. In the presence of love, there are no disguises.

2749. Is Freud alone among physicians in emphasizing the healthful benefits of love?

2750. Life without love is a contradiction.

2751. Lifelong relationships of love see beyond the
perfect facade to the endearing wrinkles within.

2752. Love at first sight is chemistry, and love at last
sight is alchemy.

2753. Love based on appearance alone is badly flawed.

2754. Love can be evil, and hatred can be virtuous.

2755. Love can never be satisfied or overdone.

2756. Love deeply enough, and we believe the
unbelievable.

2757. Love does not need or want variety; it is devotion
incarnate.

2758. Love found on the printed page
is reborn in every age.

2759. Love: hearts joined together in sweet unrest.

2760. Love in youth is drenched in fire,
burns bright with passion strong.
Love in age, more than desire,
is all there is erelong.

2761. Love is beauty with the timeless grace
of deep devotion beyond the aging face.
So close, they seem to breathe a single breath,
pray for a love beyond the touch of death.

2762. Love is more than bread and butter,
more than things to please the eye.
Without love we discover
it doesn't matter when we die.

2763. Love is not an unqualified good. A dictator's love of power is pure evil.

2764. Love is pure vulnerability.

2765. Love is the only place where joy
can ask for nothing more.
Love is a part more than the whole
that makes our spirits soar
with hopes of evermore.

2766. Love is the only place where life rises above the struggle to survive.

2767. Love is the quicksand that anchors us to life.

2768. Love only wishes to be loved.

2769. Love's appetite is without limit, but it can be satisfied with a fervent glance.

2770. Love's exclusivity defines suspicion and jealousy as measures of true devotion.

2771. Love's initial attraction is rarely the basis of lifelong commitment.

2772. Love's presence is felt in the absence of self.

2773. Love, unlike her many impostors, never speaks in past tense.

2774. Many lovers should be seen as companions of convenience.

2775. Merit may not initiate love, but it is fundamental to its survival.

2776. Our capacity for love has included deeds that are anything but lovely.

2777. People who propose unconditional love rarely mention the utter depravity of some of those they would embrace.

2778. Pray that love remains untested, for that means life is going well.

2779. Prolonged proximity puts love to the test by introducing the lovers.

2780. Real love, not found in the poet's verse, is a commitment of time and emotion few can embrace.

2781. Secret love will find its sorrow
amid the stones marked with love.
Do not wait until tomorrow;
show your heart to those above.

2782. Self-preservation is the rule
of life's amoral way;
self-sacrifice is the jewel
of love's résumé.

2783. She is the vision of delight
first in my mind both day and night;
no way to pass the livelong day
without deep love to lead the way.

2784. Some find impermanence a reason not to love. I say life without love is pointless.

2785. Some love with limits, others for all time.

2786. The alloy of love and money succumbs to the slightest stress.

2787. The faults of those we truly love have a peculiar charm.

2788. The locket worn through years apart
speaks of love more than mere art.

2789. The miracle of primordial chemistry is not life, but love.

2790. The only joy that's deep and true
is found in love's embrace.
All other ways are simply days
that pointlessly displace
life's only source of grace.

2791. The poetry of love remains aloof, untouched by the day-to-day tribulations of life.

2792. The tender touch of a hand can express the most profound feelings of love and longing.

2793. The tragedy of love is found
in final days, in hallowed ground.

2794. The writer who celebrates love addresses the only legitimate justification for this journey we call life.

2795. The world would never be the same
were she to go away;
when love is gone, there is no song
to brighten up each day—
life has lost its way.

2796. There are phone numbers never erased from our
books, for love will not die.

2797. There is a little prayer of love
I say to her each night.
No thoughts of Heaven far above
can match the lovely light
that she and I ignite!

2798. Those who love and move on have merely found
companions of convenience. True love is simply
irreplaceable.

2799. 'Tis sad to see love led astray,
embrace what's clearly wrong.
We can only hope for the day
when kindness fills the throng,
when we all belong.

2800. To cherish the faults of another is to define love.

2801. To give a reason for our love is to imply we know
ourselves far better than is likely to be true.

2802. To give reasons for love is to predict its demise.

2803. Time challenges all that we hold dear,
every moment gone forever, every hope turned to fear.
I reject the raging currents of never-ending strife,
found the reason for existence in the love of my life.

2804. To Joselita:
Your sweetness is love's delight,
your faults are cherished too,
for love is blessed with second sight
that knows the real you
whose heart is ever true.

2805. To love all is to embrace unspeakable evil.

2806. Loving humanity requires limited contact with
the species.

2807. To love truly, we must love others as they are, not
as we would like them to be.

2808. To love what is evil is to discredit love.

2809. Loving with knowledge is the ultimate validation.

2810. The idea that you should love your neighbor as
yourself may be based on a false assumption.

2811. Saying no to love for the sake of love is the
ultimate sacrifice.

2812. True beauty deepens with the years;
time's wrinkles only show
that love endures, though drenched in tears
from knowing we must go.

2813. True love is always young in heart,
no matter what the age.
Quiet devotion plays its part,
no matter what the stage.

2814. True love is not confined to youth;
it's brighter still with age.
White hair and wrinkled skin bring truth
that time alone can gauge.

2815. Wanton love is not love at all;
'tis sex dressed in protocol.

2816. We are admonished to love our neighbor which
is to accept the absurd notion that we are to base
love on geography.

2817. We recognize impermanence as nature's theme,
yet we love with an intensity that belongs to the
eternal.

2818. We run life's trying gauntlet
and finally come to see
the only thing that matters
is love's alchemy.

2819. What chance has romance in a world where men
are captivated by beauty and women are seduced
by power?

2820. What we love defines us with uncompromising
clarity, for it is tied to our deepest needs.

2821. When love is fed by desire or ambition, it should
go by some other name.

2822. When time is running out, our only thoughts are of love.

2823. When we honor the wishes of the dead, we keep love alive.

2824. When we love, proclaiming our love is not optional.

2825. When writing of the loss of love,
    tears flow as though to say
    the truest rhyme, though sublime,
    can never quite portray
    loss with us every day.

2826. Wisdom knows that life is love and all the rest is biochemistry.

2827. With introspection, it is easier to love others than it is to love ourselves.

2828. Without love, there is no more than biochemistry.

2829. Writers persist in celebrating love without ever revealing the object of love. There are many who love to do harm.

Loyalty

2830. Loyalty's devotion to the dark side is no virtue.

Luck

2831. Good luck without discipline is ruinous.

2832. Good luck may favor the intelligent, but intelligence is a matter of luck.

2833. Pluck is said to replace luck until fate finds us.

2834. The best of luck can find its way
to fools who find a rainy day
in all they see, come what may.

2835. Those who claim credit for who and what they are are willfully oblivious to vital circumstances beyond control.

2836. Those who say clean living and hard work prevent bad luck ignore the potential disasters arising from our DNA and accidental encounters with catastrophe.

Luxury

2837. Luxury in old age is not to be maligned.

2838. Experiencing luxury in youth is pure jeopardy.

Madness

2839. Shared madness is often seen as sanity.

Majority

2840. The majority is self-interest magnified. It cares little for injustice that abounds.

Marketing

2841. If you build a better mousetrap, it will be ignored without proper or improper promotion.

Marriage

2842. A government interested in protecting its citizens might reconsider the legality of marriage.

2843. Gays should be encouraged to marry as a means of furthering their education.

2844. In my case, marriage is beautiful and true, for it is based on adoration.

2845. It is likely that discretion would prevail if the price of a marriage license were comparable to the cost of a divorce decree.

2846. Love that needs a contract
to verify its bliss
often has a lawyer
bestow the final kiss.

2847. Marriage that continues in distant proximity is divorce incognito.

2848. Marriage has been known to signal the capture of prey and the death of love.

2849. Marriage is a contract that puts love in chains.

2850. Marriage: government interference in a private affair.

2851. Marriage says "I must," but love says "I will."

2852. Priests should wed indeed, for the quickest path to celibacy is marriage.

2853. The attainment of wealth through marriage is considered honorable as compared to a more direct marketing strategy.

2854. The legality of marriage subjects love to law, where disputes are the order of the day.

2855. The more importance we attach to marriage, the less importance we apply to love.

2856. The poetry of courting and the prose of marriage—how we wish it could be otherwise.

2857. Those marriages most likely to last are blessed with the sacrament of submission.

2858. Those priests who hear confessions and perform marriage ceremonies should, in good conscience, inform impending newlyweds of the lurking face of infidelity.

2859. We love our friends and marry our lovers, and occasionally, they are one.

2860. When marriage is the result of a threat of
departure, it is a matter more of law than of love.

Masks

2861. Our masks draw attention to features that would
otherwise be ignored. They reveal who we are.

Mathematics

2862. Mathematics maps an ever-changing reality
beyond the grasp of ordinary language.

2863. When this exacting discipline
steps out into the world,
it becomes a flawed paladin,
for truth is sadly swirled.
The certainty that was so prized
is math's Achilles' heel,
for the cosmos is our surmise—
confronted with the real.

2864. Since we are part of nature, perhaps it is
not surprising that our apparent creation of
mathematics is more correctly a discovery.

2865. Math's certainty is confined to human thought.
The moment it steps out into the world, it
confronts the approximations of ignorance.

2866. Mathematics strives to overcome the limitations
of perception.

2867. Mathematics substitutes patterns and predictability for insight.

2868. Reason steps its way to mathematical truth untouched by circumstantial reality.

2869. The sweep of mathematics
is metaphysics to the core,
a linguistic labyrinth
of deep metaphor.

2870. The logical rigor of mathematics dispassionately steps its way to proof.

2871. Mathematics creates its own world of postulates, definitions, and theorems. Its abstract meanderings have been known to shed light on the world outside our heads.

2872. Perhaps mathematics comes closest to the reality we never see.

2873. There is poetry in mathematics that can be written only in the precise meter of logical proof, where beauty is found in the austerity of a theorem.

2874. Mathematics is the verse of the universe.

Maturity

2875. Maturity can be measured by the number of errors we acknowledge.

Maxims

2876. A beautifully written maxim remains cold and austere till it hangs on the hooks of experience.

2877. To distill experience into memorable maxims is to make life's lessons available to all.

Meaning

2878. Goals, however inane, make life worth living.

2879. I find meaning in love and the pursuit of truth.

2880. It requires faith to address *the* meaning of life.

2881. Maturity can be measured by the number of errors we acknowledge.

2882. Some bring meaning to our momentary existence without dropping to their knees in worship.

2883. The meaning we attach to life may be false, but it serves to sustain us.

2884. The meaning we find is within us.

2885. Finding no lasting purpose in all we see is merely admitting ignorance.

2886. We can value our life greatly while believing our race will vanish with no trace.

2887. We must ignore much of the world around us to give meaning to life.

Meanness

2888. The best response to meanness is silence, for it takes center stage.

Means

2889. Test: should one who kills the killer of innocents be embraced as a moral being?

2890. The morality of the means determines the morality of the ends.

Medicine

2891. As much as one may malign the medical profession, among its practitioners are some truly great human beings.

2892. There are none who deserve our respect more than the kind and loving souls of the medical profession.

Mediocrity

2893. Diligence alone cannot deliver us from mediocrity.

2894. Mediocrity is prized when real worth is unknown or nonexistent.

2895. The clearly mediocre student may surprise the world with the genius of dedication.

Meetings

2896. Being forced to share ideas before copyright is simply tyranny.

Melancholy

2897. Melancholy equips one to confront a world that does not care.

2898. Melancholy is truth we deliberately deny.

2899. Melancholy sees present beauty in a future state of decay.

Memoirs

2900. The written word is made to serve the ego on command.

Memory

2901. A bad memory is a good friend.

2902. A memory can imbue the past with perfection, making the present ordinary at best.

2903. A poor memory blesses those with a painful life.

2904. A poor memory facilitates a clear conscience.

2905. A well-remembered past does not protect us from indomitable impulses.

2906. Forgotten memories are those phantoms that hide in the shadows and shape our lives.

2907. Imaginative memory fills the past with what might have been.

2908. Is repeatedly retelling the details of a story to the same person a sign of a poor memory?

2909. Memory defines our life to the extent that it preserves the past.

2910. Memory dresses moments with meaning.

2911. Memory evokes a creative portrait of the past.

2912. Memory is best mastered with machines, while our judgments define us.

2913. Memory is our reality not subject to revision.

2914. Memory may enhance or disappoint; its allegiance is to our personal reality, colored by a worldview as unique as our DNA.

2915. Memory measures before it stores.

2916. Memory prepares the past for publication.

2917. Memory recalls what it must believe.

2918. One with a great memory is often confined to the thoughts of others. Without recall, you must think for yourself.

2919. Past pains are recalled with ease, whereas beautiful moments vanish with no trace.

2920. Perfect memory is perfect pain.

2921. The achievements of youth grow with each passing year.

2922. The saddest days reveal that memory holds on with heart and soul.

2923. The timeless torment of painful memories makes the prospect of memory loss inviting.

2924. Those who recall a past full of departed loved ones live in a diminished present.

2925. Those with a great memory are rarely memorable.

2926. Time cannot erase moments of grace or disgrace. The past is part of who we are.

2927. Time shapes recollections to serve our needs.

2928. Time tears memory into pieces that unite into a fabric of will and desire that bears some resemblance to actual events.

2929. We remember best what we would forget.

Men and Women

2930. A man's car and a woman's makeup present a face to the world.

2931. The greater civility of women may vanish in a truly free society.

Mercy

2932. Mercy without limits brings justice to its knees.

Merit

2933. If you wish to be thought worthy, you must not stray very far from the constraints of culture.

2934. Love's chemistry finds merit inert.

2935. Merit is always a matter of favoritism.

2936. Merit should not be defined
by currency's precious seal.
Real worth is virgin birth
with a touch of the surreal?

Metaphysics

2937. Metaphysics has found a home in the abstract formulations of mathematics.

Mind

2938. Borrowed brains are often found
the way to make our own
soar so high they do astound
those who receive the loan;
no greatness stands alone.

2939. Many convert "if A, then B" to B with no need
of A.

2940. The mind can be a retreat from the
incomprehensible world of our senses.

2941. The mind defines our life
with happiness or strife.

Minorities

2942. Minorities challenge the status quo
with all that heart and mind can sow,
but when they reach majority rule,
no more of thought; just play the fool

Minute

2943. This precious minute now appears,
none like it in the past.
Must savor that which disappears
into life's fluid cast
where nothing's made to last.

Miracles

2944. It is not uncommon to confuse the
incomprehensible with the miraculous.

2945. Miracles are seen as God's fireworks, dazzling his
subjects into mindless adoration.

2946. The mysterious restoration of health reveals our
ignorance, not the existence of God.

2947. Those who invoke the divine when confronted
with the inexplicable have embraced the comfort
of belief.

Mischief

2948. Gold may not reach for what is right
for wherewithal may delight
in mischief in the dead of night;
seems our nature's grievous plight.

Miser

2949. The miser feels no heartbeat of romance but
knows only the golden coffin he calls life.

Misery

2950. Misery may be in the mind, but it is enhanced by little or no means of support.

2951. Misery sees happiness in death.

Misfortune

2952. Loss of those we love stays with us still;
time will not heal, nor act of will.

2953. The misfortunes hardest to bear always occur.

2954. Those who say the worst misfortunes never occur have never loved.

Mistake

2955. Two wrongs may set you right.

Moderation

2956. Moderation in pursuit of virtue is a vice.

2957. Moderation is the path to mediocrity.

2958. The moderation of the powerless is no virtue.

Modesty

2959. Modest gifts have no need of modesty, and great gifts are not concealed by it.

2960. Modesty apologizes for life's inequities.

2961. Modesty that denies true excellence chooses acceptance over truth.

2962. The mediocre find status in modesty.

Money

2963. Money converts conscience into a commodity subject to market fluctuations.

2964. Money gives us time to write,
to think without duress;
work's bondage gone—out of sight,
words come and we profess.

2965. Money has been demonized
by writers who pretend
that luxuries are despised
by those who comprehend—
pretentious to the end.

2966. Money is the means that lays bare the amoral impulses of its victims.

2967. Money rules when fools have the misfortune of a windfall.

2968. Money tests our principles with mathematical precision.

2969. No mansion is large enough to conceal the smallness of its occupants.

2970. The real value of money is revealed by what money cannot buy.

2971. When a wealthy man buys a beautiful woman, both are corrupted.

Mood

2972. Moods can mold feeling and thought into memorable lines of verse.

2973. Moods may be understood but never changed by logic.

Morality

2974. A beloved president with several mistresses reveals our moral relativity.

2975. A clear conscience may see its way to murder and mayhem. Comfort is not a measure of goodness.

2976. A clear conscience may see its way to the dark door of "anything goes."

2977. A dishonest world finds discreet falsehood an endearing trait.

2978. A morality founded on kindness has no need of religious doctrine.

2979. A morality that would sacrifice the few to save the many is based on mathematics. This view makes homicide a virtue.

2980. Avoiding evil is not the same as doing good.

2981. Being well-educated often contributes more to wealth than to morality. Simple goodness is rarely found in the curriculum.

2982. Belief in goodness is not belief in God.

2983. Betrayal's first victim is the betrayer.

2984. Both pride and shame define our morality.

2985. Both valor and honesty can and often do serve nefarious ends.

2986. Can one pledge allegiance to both country and conscience?

2987. Character can fail and find joy in the journey.

2988. Character—not happiness, wealth, or position—should command our respect.

2989. Considering human nature, feeling good is clearly not a measure of morality.

2990. Considering our penchant for depravity, self-control is our only salvation.

2991. Contingent morality is pure expediency.

2992. Disappointment with humanity lies in its potential for virtue.

2993. Even kindness can be immoral.

2994. Fine distinctions are a scoundrel's first line of defense.

2995. Good is found in deeds alone,
not praying for what's right.
Begging will not bring backbone
needed in the night.

2996. Goodness can be sad, and happiness can be evil.

2997. Goodness is to be admired even if there is no impulse to be bad.

2998. Great deeds sometimes grow from seeds of shame.

2999. Hitler's intellectuals revealed that academic excellence can be dangerously amoral.

3000. Honesty is full of spines, while deceit is smooth as silk.

3001. If a human being or supreme being fails to help those in distress and has the power to do so, then the question of character arises.

3002. If moral relativity
is absolutely true,
then right and wrong both belong
to everything we do.

3003. If the morality of an act is dependent on motive,
then anything goes.

3004. If there are no absolute standards of morality,
then good and evil become the playthings of
philosophy.

3005. If we find no one worthy of respect, we reveal
who and what we are.

3006. If you find no shame in your thoughts, you are
clearly amoral.

3007. In mathematics and morality, postulates point
the way.

3008. It is far easier to follow a bad example than to
civilize our human nature.

3009. Kindness in the abstract may seem to be pure
goodness until bestowed upon a serial killer.

3010. Morality arises from the human mind, as
does God.

3011. Morality based on authority may have little to do
with right and wrong.

3012. Morality embracing self-defense makes war
inevitable.

3013. Morality is love of doing right, not fear of doing wrong.

3014. One's true character cannot escape the revealing lens of laughter.

3015. One who is omnipotent and allows pain and suffering to prevail is without morality.

3016. Only the amoral have nothing to hide.

3017. One tires of the bigotry
of clerics far and wide;
decency does not require
a deity to decide.

3018. Opposing moralities are thought to be absolutely true.

3019. Poverty is likely to give law and order a low priority.

3020. Poverty's crimes are petty, whereas wealth transgresses on a grand scale.

3021. Principles are showcased while practice is misplaced.

3022. Reflecting on human nature reveals the danger of becoming all that you can be.

3023. Religious morality is sustained through fear of an omnipotent being and the promise of eternal life.

3024. Reward and punishment are sound principles of commerce, not morality.

3025. Reward taints virtuous conduct with a bargain.

3026. Saints with a passion
for life's many treats
are rarer than sinners
seeking a retreat.

3027. Salvation puts all virtue in jeopardy.

3028. Some murder in the name of morality.

3029. The approval of society at large should not be confused with virtue.

3030. The conflict between morals and money rarely ends in poverty.

3031. The delusion that beauty is virtue requires little experience to dismiss.

3032. The evolution of wants serves to define us.

3033. The alleged immorality of prostitution pales in the presence of churchly misconduct.

3034. The impulse to despise ourselves gives one hope.

3035. The insights of genius pale in the presence of a charitable act.

3036. The jokes that offend serve to define our character.

3037. The more we cling to some higher authority to manage our lives, the more we see fear as the foundation of morality.

3038. The notion that being loving and kind is related to belief in a personal God contradicts our experience.

3039. The philanthropist who signs his name seeks to make pride a virtue.

3040. The religious claim morality as their own while they worship an omnipotent God who refuses to prevent the wanton cruelty that abounds.

3041. The rich who obey the law embrace prosperity and perhaps morality.

3042. The rivalry of adults reveals the infancy of the race.

3043. The salvation of the moral atheist is found in goodness, not godliness.

3044. There are better reasons to be good than religion.

3045. There are those who would promote genocide in the name of morality.

3046. There are virtues of omission as well as commission.

3047. There is more than a trace of immorality in doing good to achieve salvation.

3048. Those who call evil a sickness create a defense for the most despicable behavior.

3049. Those who do good with no expectation of reward are irreligious.

3050. Those who do good without belief in a personal God or the expectation of reward define what it means to be moral.

3051. Those who favor survival of the fittest celebrate the amoral dominance of those who are more able.

3052. Those who preach fair play often have a winning hand.

3053. Those who speak of a realistic approach to life do not allow principle to interfere with practice.

3054. Associating atheism with vice is as absurd as allying theism with virtue.

3055. Getting along by going along is pure amorality.

3056. To get even is to follow a bad example.

3057. Loving a profoundly evil enemy is not a virtue.

3058. Loving those who hate us means the Jews should love Hitler.

3059. That evils are transitory is irrelevant to those who perish in their path.

3060. To reject divine salvation and live a virtuous life is to be truly moral.

3061. To reject human nature is to embrace morality.

3062. Seeing war as a legitimate means to advancement is pure amorality.

3063. To stay alive at any cost is to betray everyone, including yourself.

3064. To the moral relativist any act can embrace good or evil. It is only a matter of perspective.

3065. Traitors have loyalties.

3066. Travel the world and find virtue and vice in an identity crisis.

3067. Unqualified moral imperatives rarely survive critical analysis.

3068. Virtue becomes vice when it is adopted merely as effective strategy.

3069. Virtue is not so well-defined
as some are prone to say;
born in the fertile human mind,
can change with time of day.

3070. Virtue vanishes into the amoral realm of the popular, where anything goes.

3071. Virtue's tenure is brief when found on the ballot.

3072. Votes are more likely to express self-interest than virtue. A voting majority should not define our morality, and the welfare of all should be our goal.

3073. We are defined by our treatment of strangers.

3074. We arose from the primordial soup, and our greatest achievement is morality.

3075. We use our morality for kindness and killing.

3076. When chance favors the few over the many, some would decide to interfere to establish equality. The principles of morality, unlike those of physics, are our creation.

3077. When morality moves from the abstract to the particular, it takes on the tincture of the times.

3078. When someone says, "I'm only human," anything goes.

3079. When we are the exception, our morality is suspect.

3080. When will the coveted prize of ambition be kindness?

Morality and Religion

3081. One should not confuse morality with religion. The religious do not adore virtue.

Mortality

3082. Our survival as a species is dependent on our mortality.

3083. What terrifies is the dust-filled reality of oblivion.

Motives

3084. A close examination of motives puts the best
actions in jeopardy.

3085. Motives lie in the shadows,
giving rise to what we do.
Our actions and reactions
may never give a clue.

3086. Motives usually transcend the mere impulse to do
good.

3087. Motives wander freely, crossing moral boundaries
as they go.

Music

3088. I worked on the Bach Inventions relentlessly,
revealing that love and hard work do not
necessarily lead to excellence.

Mystery

3089. What we consider obvious, when seen with a
philosophic eye, is full of mystery.

Mythology

3090. Mythology sustains many at the expense of truth.

3091. Our fear-driven mythologies bring solace and chaos in the quest for eternal life.

Name

3092. An object is not more real or understandable because we assign it a name.

3093. Beyond mere identification, we name things to feel we know and possess them.

3094. Names identify with confidence an underlying reality unknown and unknowable.

3095. When we say we know the name of something, there is the implication that the name was always there.

Natural

3096. When we embrace the natural, we must include war and pestilence.

Natural Selection

3097. A morality that is designed for survival would never choose to do the right thing and perish.

3098. A religion that promises salvation is fully consistent with natural selection.

3099. Despite its survival value, the human race has been reluctant to adopt morality as an imperative.

3100. It is difficult to see morality arise from natural selection when the strong dominate the weak.

3101. Morality is fully consistent with natural selection when it chooses to die in this life to enter the next.

3102. Natural selection, by its very nature, chooses survival over virtue.

3103. Since we are part of nature, it can be argued that we naturally select morality for its survival value.

3104. Survival by any means is nature's way.

3105. Survival is the golden rule
of life's eternal quest,
the fist alone the cornerstone
of defining all with zest
till extinction lays to rest.

Nature

3106. Are nature's endless cycles of birth and death worthy of our love?

3107. Has nature selected intelligence to end all life?

3108. It is sad to note that nowhere in terrestrial nature has kindness been adopted as a pervasive principle of survival.

3109. Nature robs us of our powers till all that's left is thought.

3110. Nature's face changes constantly in the heartless pursuit of what?

3111. One wonders whether life on other worlds has found a peaceful path to survival.

3112. Some find congenital impulses too powerful to overcome and conclude that what is natural is right.

3113. The multitude of deadly phenomena that permeate the cosmos inspires fear where ignorance once found beauty.

3114. To glorify nature unconditionally is to cherish the brutal struggle for existence.

3115. We have become nature's contradiction by creating morality, which is simply unnatural.

Necessity

3116. Courage can be confused with necessity.

3117. Culture promotes its own necessities that define its world.

3118. How many Christians find it necessary to die rather than kill in what is called self-defense?

3119. Many call on necessity to legitimize desire.

3120. Necessity is called upon to defend war, never to defend peace.

3121. Necessity is merely obstacles not yet overcome.

3122. There is freedom in necessity, for it requires no choice to be made.

3123. Those in power preach necessity as a way of making the shackles of government tolerable.

Need

3124. For me, love is the transcending need that puts all other wants in perspective.

3125. Needs define us and sometimes destroy us.

3126. Those who invoke God when they want something are not likely to get it.

3127. To not need other people is to know nothing of love.

Neighbor

3128. To choose one's neighbors as companions only because they are neighbors is to be without discrimination.

Neutrality

3129. Neutrality in the end may save lives, for every war is replete with atrocity.

3130. Neutrality may merely be an unwillingness to fight.

3131. Neutrality may see and support the wisdom of Christ.

3132. The neutrality of the heart is found only in death.

3133. Those who remain neutral in the face of profound evil have few rivals among barbarians.

Newness

3134. Newness is often mistaken for artistry.

Newton and Einstein

3135. Natural law revealed by Newton's touch
brought forth approval that he knew so much,
explained his world with elegance supreme
till Einstein broke the spell. As from a dream,
a world without bearings tossed and turned all night,
truth ever sought, forever out of sight.

New Year

3136. Each New Year, we endure hope's contest with reality.

3137. We say "Happy New Year" to all
while knowing a sad truth;
the celebration's protocol
finds life a stern reproof.

Night

3138. The writer finds the dead of night
alive with thought sublime;
the darkness seems to shed a light
that lingers for all time.

Noise

3139. The lights and sounds of the casino never interrupt my stream of thoughts.

Nonsense

3140. The nonsense of the famous is cherished by the thoughtless.

Nonviolence

3141. Human beings have found nonviolence inconsistent with their nature; perhaps in time we will evolve.

3142. Nature's motif is full of violence. The fact that we conceive of nonviolence is a step forward.

Normality

3143. A moment's reflection will reveal that normality is something to overcome.

3144. Each culture defines what is normal unambiguously. To be normal is to conform.

3145. Normal citizens proudly kill for God and country, while the abnormal, who refuse to kill, are censured for thoughtful disobedience.

3146. The mathematics of normality suggests it is more normal to kill than to write.

3147. There appears to be more self-interest than kindness in a normal human being.

3148. Though normality is an abstraction never to be seen in any one person, the impulse to prevail appears to be pervasive.

3149. To praise normality in the light of human behavior is dubious at best.

Nothing

3150. Can we conceive of nothing and exist?

Novelty

3151. The novel sparkles with newness, blinding us to established excellence.

Objects

3152. The cost of an object seduces us into seeing beauty apart from its intrinsic value.

Oblivion

3153. All of my books are a reply to oblivion.

3154. Passion is extraordinary indeed when it is sustained while contemplating the oblivion that confronts us all.

Obscurity

3155. It's not so bad to be the one
few can call by name,
for nothing here is made to last,
including precious fame.

3156. Obscurity saves us from reproach and denies us appreciation.

Observation

3157. A careful observer who sees how life plays out may limit his participation.

3158. Our observations are an admixture of observer and observed. What we see is colored by who and what we are.

3159. Our observations are often filtered by preconceptions that prevent us from seeing anything of significance.

Obvious

3160. The problem with the "obvious" is that what is clear to some is incomprehensible to others.

Open Mind

3161. A truly open mind is amoral, for our penchant for evil is ever present.

3162. An open mind can embrace sense and nonsense with equal ease.

Opinions

3163. If we reject opinions we wish were true, we are thoughtful indeed.

3164. Joys uninfluenced by the opinions of others are true indeed.

3165. Perfect argument can be false, and offhand opinion can be true.

3166. Poor arguments can undermine the most astute opinions.

3167. The need to believe makes all popular opinion suspect.

Optimism

3168. Ignorance is the most reliable source of optimism.

3169. It is prudent to live optimistically, with the understanding that stars die.

3170. Optimism converts an amoral and ugly world into a haven of wish fulfillment.

3171. Optimism defies the inevitable.

3172. Optimism is a triumph of hope that for a time enriches experience.

3173. Optimism is assured of future failure.

3174. Optimism sheds its own light.

3175. The deception of optimism is unreasonably wise.

3176. The present denies optimism a foothold.
Optimism flourishes in a fanciful future where all
experience is set aside.

Optimism and Pessimism

3177. Optimism is useful, but pessimism is inevitable.
Why embrace truth when falsehood sustains us?

3178. The optimist claims the best is yet to come,
whereas the pessimist knows the best is a prelude
to disaster.

3179. The optimist creates a world the pessimist never
sees.

3180. The wealthy pessimist is difficult to ignore. He
has what we want, yet he remains on the dark
side.

Oratory

3181. Oratory that is considered great is rarely logically
compelling.

3182. Oratory requires simple formulas to reach and
hold the audience spellbound.

Order

3183. Can it be that our need for order prevents us from seeing underlying chaos?

3184. To say chance reflects ignorance, we must believe in order.

Ordinary People

3185. One wonders whether those who refer to ordinary people ever include themselves in the rubric.

Originality

3186. Every authoritative doctrine finds the original mind an adversary.

3187. It has been said that nature never invented the wheel. Are we not part of nature?

Orthodoxy

3188. The orthodox is often maligned even when the new is an abomination.

Others

3189. The self alone is pure emptiness. A vital *other* is, for me, the reason to be.

3190. If we don't nourish others, we starve.

Ought

3191. "Ought" is not well-defined.

Pacifism

3192. An absolute pacifist is maligned for the dangerous principle of nonviolence.

3193. We conceive of pacifism for human survival while we choose war for mutual annihilation.

Paradox

3194. After a lifetime of study, the most profound insight is seen in the admission of ignorance.

3195. The paradox shows that logic's power is more symbolic than real.

Parents

3196. Our parents did their very best
with what they came to know;
brought many laws along with flaws
to show us how to go;
some few were apropos.

Particular

3197. The particular, with its inherent complexity,
lacks the elegance of the abstract truth that it
engenders.

Parting

3198. Parting is the doorway to sorrow.

Passion

3199. In argument, passion often supports the
unsupportable.

3200. Passion is primal and rarely evolves beyond the
impulse to prevail.

3201. Passionate goals are best reached dispassionately.

3202. The conclusions of passion are above reproach;
they may be wrong, but they are full of integrity.

3203. The more passionate the preacher, the more
untenable the argument.

3204. The passion that inspires a writer must be
subdued by discipline that allows true artistry to
emerge.

Past

3205. Each moment now becomes the past,
no matter what we do.
We wish for some to last and last
when love is sweet and true.

3206. My past seems replete with circumstances that
dominate as much by chance as by choice. So
many events that seemed trivial at the time were
truly momentous.

3207. The past haunts every waking hour,
cannot be put away—
the more we live, the more we give
to memories' melee—
"if only" has its say.

3208. To study the past is to know that repetition is the
theme of life.

3209. We're all made to repeat the past,
for nature does not lie.
Born with a plan, a telling strand
of DNA to try.

3210. What appears to be the same past evolves into so many personas; DNA ultimately prevails.

Patience

3211. Patience allows purpose to prevail.

3212. Patience can serve many masters. One can patiently pursue evil.

3213. Patience puts mere talent in its place; it is more in tune with genius.

Patriotism

3214. Armed with patriotism, no atrocity is without justification.

3215. One who holds country above loved ones has chosen an abstraction over love.

3216. Patriotism is the amoral pursuit of victory in the name of God and country.

3217. The patriot loves to hate.

3218. Those who love patriotism must passionately embrace the followers of Adolf Hitler.

Peace

3219. Each nation recognizes its own lack of integrity, and this forms the basis of distrust that abounds.

3220. Intelligent machines may someday keep the peace.

3221. Lasting peace is possible only when *their* interests are as important as *our* interests.

3222. Many of us live in prisons where the space above the entryway is inscribed, "Peace at any price."

3223. Peace of mind can be seen in some who kill thousands.

3224. Peace will remain out of reach so long as we extend to ourselves the right to bear arms.

3225. The oligarchs of so-called democracy reject peace in pursuit of profit.

3226. The Swiss have found peace profitable.

3227. To embrace peace at any price is to welcome slavery.

3228. To have peace of mind is to ignore the world as it is.

3229. To seek peace is to deny our nature.

Perception

3230. Anatomy defines us and the world we live in.

3231. Our perceptions are, for the most part, colored by the preconceptions of our culture. Formal education most often fosters societal bias.

3232. Our world cannot be *the* world, for perception is a creative process.

3233. What would we see without language?

Perfection

3234. Even Christ had his critics.

3235. Is there anything or anyone in this world considered perfect by all?

3236. Perfect behavior's flaw is never finding a rule it does not follow.

3237. What is considered perfect has no meaning apart from the culture that defines it.

Performance

3238. The admonition to do things well is problematic. There are many situations where "well done" is not well-defined.

Permanence

3239. We cherish permanence even when confronted with tyranny.

3240. We strive for permanence in a world where sunflowers and suns perish.

Perseverance

3241. Perseverance defines our limitations.

3242. Perseverance is blind to its limitations, which allows it to prevail.

3243. People who persevere may come to know that the real joy is in the striving, not the winning.

3244. Perseverance prevails within the limits of ability.

3245. To do what you love and do no harm is enough of victory.

Persuasion

3246. Fear and love serve to persuade while reason fails to make the grade.

Philanthropy

3247. Some give their wealth and not their name;
true goodness is their only aim.

3248. The proud philanthropist whose name is attached
to every gift has more fame than virtue.

3249. The philanthropist who avoids paying taxes
through loopholes reveals his true nature.

3250. Those who say it is Godlike to help others have
little experience with catastrophe.

Philosophy

3251. Insofar as a philosopher is one who seeks truth
unencumbered by cherished belief, a religious
philosopher is an oxymoron.

3252. Insofar as philosophy seeks truth, it is never out
of fashion.

3253. It is as unreasonable to worship reason as it is to
worship God.

3254. If you embrace doubt without depression, you are
a philosopher.

3255. Philosophy becomes religion when it embraces a
personal God.

3256. Philosophy is focused on fundamental questions
and is fully aware that all answers are tentative.

3257. Philosophy seeks truth that transcends the passing certainties of every age.

3258. Philosophy teaches us to challenge cherished belief.

3259. Philosophy: the infinitesimal embracing infinity.

3260. The deeper philosophy goes, the more it replaces doctrine with doubt.

3261. To question manifest truth is to be a philosopher.

Physics

3262. Einstein's notion that motion through space affects the passage of time is a prime example of a nonintuitive idea.

Plagiarism

3263. The thought may be old, but the line should be unforgettable.

Play

3264. In my later years, writing thoughts in prose and poetry is the play I enjoy the most.

Pleasures

3265. A writer is reluctant to finish a book, for when the work is done, all that remains is the unsatisfying pursuit of pleasure.

3266. For the writer, the pleasure of crafting a well-written line has few competitors.

3267. Pleasures define us, for they are unable to lie.

3268. Satisfying hunger for food easily competes with the pleasure of writing a poem. Our pleasures have no natural hierarchy but serve the needs of the moment.

Poetry

3269. A critic is quick to malign a poet who seeks truth.

3270. A profound sense of wonder finds a home in the pensive meanderings of a poet's pen.

3271. Few modern poets can write with the clarity, insight, and mathematical precision of Pope.

3272. Frost said it best of all
when discussing free verse.
Tennis played with no net
is simply perverse.

3273. Great poetry can be brilliantly clear or subtly mysterious, but it is always memorable.

3274. I asked several well-educated people to find unforgettable lines in the work of twenty-first-century prize-winning free-verse poets. They found none.

3275. I would rather have written "Sea Fever" than captain any ship.

3276. It is no surprise that few modern poets can compose well on command.

3277. My songs may triumph over death,
or so it seems in dead of night,
when thoughts emerge with bated breath
of hopes and dreams that shed their light
and then fade quickly out of sight.

3278. Poetry at its best
brings feelings to the fore.
Lines are etched in memory's breast
for now and evermore.

3279. Poetry can embrace abstract thought as readily as deep feelings; it is a genre for the human experience.

3280. Poetry is always a passion, for it expects no worldly reward.

3281. Poetry is best when truth is enhanced by beauty.

3282. Poetry that fails to create a beautiful marriage of sense and sound has failed.

3283. Poetry transcends mere music for it has both music and subtle thought.

3284. Premonition is the poet's realm; it is sight without light.

3285. Rhymes are the fair weather of literature.

3286. The artistry required to write in meter and rhyme is ignored by those moderns who embrace the easy meanderings of would-be verse.

3287. The descriptive prose of modern poetry carefully avoids profound thought and the creative synthesis of sense and sound.

3288. The poet's privacy is assured by a society that rarely reads verse.

3289. The simple words of verse reveal
what we think and how we feel;
they speak to all of love and life,
hope for a moment's end to strife.

3290. The undisciplined ramblings of free verse mark the death of poetry.

3291. Those who favor free verse talk of the tyranny of rhyme, but great poets make rhyme unforgettable.

3292. Thoughts and feelings are transformed by poetry into something unforgettable that becomes part of our repertoire.

3293. To admire the perfection of Pope is to be perfectly out of step with current taste.

3294. We write our verse in blood at first; life dealt us every line.

3295. What passes for verse,
    assaulting my mind,
    is unworthy of a race
    spawning Keats and his kind.

3296. Writing poetry allows—no, requires—an
    evolution of thought not found in prose. I am
    never quite sure how it will end.

Poetry and Art

3297. Art now consists of pouring paint on a canvas,
    and poetry has become no more than poor prose,
    with no hint of the artistry that once thrilled
    thousands.

Politics

3298. A politician who speaks of his religion is not to be
    trusted.

3299. A politician with integrity serves a single term.

3300. A successful politician rarely has trouble deciding
    between money and morality.

3301. If the president of a country were to begin a
    speech with "I was wrong," it would herald a new
    era in politics.

3302. The lies of politics reflect priorities of candidates
    and the electorate. Truth is simply intolerable.

3303. The political leader who believes in nothing has the flexibility to prevail.

3304. The vulgarity of a candidate buys the weightless votes of a majority.

3305. Those poor uneducated citizens who vote for those who favor the rich reveal the value of an education.

3306. Virtue's tenure is brief when found on the ballot.

Popularity

3307. Popularity sought is identity lost.

Possessions

3308. Possessions never satisfy
a burden of desire;
the more we get,
the more we want,
lost in what we acquire.

3309. Possessions are companions that never satisfy. The only benefit is an ever-growing economy.

3310. Possessions possess, 'tis true;
they hold us in their spell.
But none can give or forgive
as lovers do so well—
just things for show and tell.

3311.   The more we possess, the less we are free.

3312.   We do not possess what we cannot give away.

Possibility

3313.   If fundamental rules of reality exist, then they
        define the possible.

3314.   Possibility may be illusory, but it never fails to
        inspire.

3315.   The actual may disappoint, but the possible is
        never without hope.

3316.   The possible brings regret for paths not taken.

3317.   What might have been is never known,
        but surely fate can be
        a fickle force that can be shown
        to favor you or me—
        pure possibility.

Posterity

3318.   Bertrand Russell hoped for assurance that the
        human race would survive. Sadly, the bellicosity
        of our species, coupled with nature's many
        catastrophes, makes our long-term survival
        improbable.

3319. Our hope that the future will know better is unconvincing, for the past was once someone's future.

3320. Posterity judges what we have done, not who we are.

Postulates

3321. Assumptions bring comfortable knowledge of what must be, until we begin to think.

3322. Our assumptions confine us to the world of our own thinking.

3323. Postulates are the intuitive foundations of proof.

3324. Postulates are the pillars of our truth. They define our world.

3325. To challenge postulates is to think.

3326. What we believe without proof defines us.

Potentiality

3327. Realizing our potential as a species can be dangerous indeed, for that potential can be found anywhere on the moral continuum.

Poverty

3328. A truly civilized society would not allow poverty to exist. Those who are willing to work, even when they are unable to do so, should never be poor.

3329. Philosophy offers no consolation to the poor.

3330. Poverty promotes failure, and the few who overcome it are extraordinary indeed.

Power

3331. Few are immune to the viral potency of power. In its purest form, the kindest soul succumbs.

3332. Our need to worship is seen in our willingness to overlook the depravity of those in power.

3333. Power corrupts those who should not have it. Unfortunately, that includes most of the human race.

3334. Some find pleasure in pursuit of power and find pain in its attainment.

3335. The possession of power promotes the exercise of will, not wisdom.

3336. Those who love power are remarkably fond of themselves.

3337. To attain power is to define character.

3338. To not feel the burden of power is to have no character.

Praise

3339. If your satisfaction depends on the approval of others, then your work will be tailored to conform to prevailing taste.

3340. Lavish praise sets the stage for inevitable censure.

3341. Praise is irresistible to those whose sense of worth comes from without.

3342. Praise is rarely conferred on subtle discourse.

3343. Unearned praise is rarely corrected when we are the recipient.

Prayer

3344. Prayer can be a useful belief in the unbelievable.

3345. Prayer reflects the nature of parishioners and the God they create.

3346. The war prayer exposes religion's dark side. The loving God is asked to participate in the carnage, revealing the all-too-human nature of religious belief.

3347. To ask God to use divine power to interfere with what he has ordained is to accuse God of bad judgment.

Preaching

3348. To our chagrin, there are many among us who practice what they preach.

3349. Preaching what we practice has the redeeming value of honesty.

Precedents

3350. Precedents convince the thoughtless.

Predictions

3351. Even predictability wrapped in elegant mathematics is no guarantee of truth.

3352. The backward boy who learns to read slowly may write thoughtful books never envisioned by lads of great promise.

Prejudice

3353. A prejudice that satisfies our needs is untouched by experience.

3354. The only racial prejudice of merit is the prejudice against the human race.

Preparation

3355. If there is no event for which you cannot prepare, you have never loved.

Present

3356. No future can compete with the present when a person is in love.

3357. The precious minute now appears,
none like it in the past.
Must savor that which disappears
into life's fluid cast,
where nothing's made to last.

3358. The present constantly vanishes into the elastic medium of time; its momentary touch is what we call life.

Pride

3359. Faced with oblivion, pride is laughable.

3360. The only pride of merit denounces all pride.

3361. The proud see praise as their unique province.

3362. Admitting error openly is pride redeemed.

3363. Pride gives credit to the self alone.

3364. Humility has found a place
where pride is lurking still;
we play down our strengths with seeming grace
while seeking sweet goodwill.

3365. Speak well of yourself, and you will not be
troubled with praise from others.

3366. Pride knows nothing of chance.

3367. We proudly claim we're free of pride and quickly
hide our seamy side.

3368. We can be proud of the pride that embraces the
wisdom of others.

Principle

3369. Hard times tend to find a moral code
inconvenient, whereas prosperity embraces
principle to keep the good times rolling.

3370. Principles are the ornaments of prosperity.

3371. The anchor of principle is raised in troubled
waters.

Prizes

3372. One wonders whether those who decide who wins might be so moved by a work that they dare not confer the prize, lest it discourage future efforts. It is doubtful that this thought will bring solace to those of us who lose.

3373. Prizes are suspect when they value the new more than the substantial.

3374. The prize:
Those who have what we want
may not be what we hope;
Hemingway won the prize
and found no way to cope.

Profiling

3375. Police profile the old and gray
with kindness due those who are prey;
seems strength is seen as evil's path
to human nature full of wrath.

Progress

3376. Improvement in medical science provides more time to express our human nature.

3377. Progress: New tools and old rules.

3378. Our evolution has allowed us to express our nature with increasing effectiveness.

3379. We must ignore the genocide of the past century to believe in progress.

3380. We cannot by force of intellect evolve into better beings, for to change our nature, we must *be* something else.

3381. With humans' powerful primate brain, technical progress is a certainty, but moral progress is yet to be seen.

Promise

3382. A promise is a hope that goes up in smoke.

3383. Promises are goals tested by our ability and our resolve.

Proof

3384. Proof is always suspect, for it is based on postulates accepted without proof.

3385. Since no proof is free of assumptions, one can prove a statement is true that is perfectly false.

Propaganda

3386. Propaganda works best when it reflects our nature and reinforces our bias.

Propriety

3387. The wish to be proper often overrides our impulse to tell the truth or be ourselves.

Proverbs

3388. Proverbs are time capsules of thought.

3389. Proverbs can be fully understood only through flesh-and-blood encounters with experience.

3390. Proverbs more often strike the memory than the manners.

Providence

3391. The chores of the day may lead through a labyrinth that ends in a life-altering event. Providence will have its way.

Pulitzer

3392. Some try for the Pulitzer
with verse tied up so fine
that cries for freedom can be heard
by jurors who malign
the slightest hint of rhyme.

Puritans

3393. The puritan sees indecency in a smile,
finding the only pleasure in denial.

Purity

3394. Does purity of heart include those villains who
steadfastly pursued what they saw as admirable?

Purpose

3395. In the end, there is no essential difference between
running one of life's many races and writing
poetry.

3396. My purpose is to write and love; it is life
sustaining.

3397. Purpose can be dark, bringing joy beyond
morality.

3398. Stars are born and die each day;
we wonder why they're here.
No purpose seems to hold sway;
seems all will disappear
in the cosmos where we peer.

3399. The purpose of life or the universe is simply a matter of ignorance.

3400. The purpose we see in daily life cannot easily be extended to the universe of our acquaintance.

3401. There is cold neutrality in a life without purpose.

Quarrel

3402. We fight with ourselves when we think.

Questions

3403. Great questions may be unanswerable, but they do provoke thought.

3404. Questions become the hallmarks of wisdom.

3405. Questions can be answers in disguise.

3406. The more profound our knowledge, the more astute our questions.

3407. Those questions are best that admit no ready answers.

Quotations

3408. Books of quotations rely heavily on fame,
while wisdom looks beyond a familiar name.

3409. Fame can burden a quotation with unfulfilled
expectations.

3410. I once asked a representative of a prominent
university to consider me for inclusion in their
new book of quotations. The reply: "We only
quote the famous." Apparently, fame is the only
source of excellence.

3411. Quotations may express a thought we never had
or express our own thought in a way we never
could. In either case they serve us well.

3412. Some seek renown by finding words of note,
immortality lost with each familiar quote.

3413. Quoting is an excellent form of self-expression.

3414. When the famous borrow a line, it becomes theirs
for all time.

Race

3415. Few of us are colorblind;
we're born in a milieu.
The color we first see a kind
we choose without a clue
that virtue has no hue.

Reading

3416. Books are written for the moment or for
millennia. What do you read?

3417. Choose an author who makes you uncomfortable.

3418. If you never disagree with what is said,
you have proved to be a reader who's well led.

3419. Reading is immersion in the thoughts of others;
be careful you don't drown.

3420. Reading is the way to thought, so long as you
can't be bought.

3421. Some of us find companions in literature and find
life in thought.

3422. The best books are those that can be reread
repeatedly with benefit.

Reality

3423. A small dose of reality is all we can bear.

3424. I suspect that to see things as they are would be to
confront the chaos beyond the unifying principles
we impose on reality.

3425. If we could add a dozen senses to those we already
possess, we would not catch a glimpse of reality.

3426. Reality is ever elusive and will not be confined by
what we believe.

3427. The prime reality of the moment is the threat we
pose to human existence.

3428. To face stark reality
buys us nothing but defeat;
better to write poetry
and dream of meadows sweet.

3429. What is our reality? We are the result of the
random groupings of evolution, residing on
a speck in an unimaginably vast universe and
subject to natural forces that give vulnerability
new meaning.

Reason

3430. Our reason defines our mental reality, which *may*
relate to the world outside our head.

3431. On reason's trek to truth, the most powerful
adversary is belief.

3432. People can arrive at the same conclusion and
disagree strongly.

3433. Reason and passion are more likely to be foes than
friends.

3434. Reason, at its best, sees its own shortcomings.

3435. Reason consists of rules of thought that we violate as the need arises.

3436. Reason is an unpopular interloper in the world of passionate belief. We prefer comfortable lies to unpalatable truth.

3437. Reason is more persuasive with machines than with men.

3438. Reason is summoned to validate belief. When it fails, we dismiss it as an unfaithful servant.

3439. Reason's fallibility lies in its assumptions.

3440. Reason should not be confused with truth; it is nothing more than a logical process. Begin with false premises, and you will draw false conclusions.

3441. Teachers of geometry, with their immersion in logical thought, seem to be out of place in a world where conclusions precede proof.

3442. The "if then" syntax of reason is at odds with imagination.

3443. Saying that belief in a personal God concerned with our welfare has a rational basis reveals reluctance to abandon reason in pursuit of the unreasonable.

3444. When reason leaves the sanctuary of mathematics, it confronts the worldly agenda of the real, where logic may be one of the many paths to truth.

Reason and Causality

3445. God denies causality and puts reason in a quandary.

3446. Reason fails when we insist that every effect has a cause.

3447. The finest telescope fails to find the first cause.

Recompense

3448. The crucified Christ forgave those who were killing him, and then he was killed.

3449. The notion that kindness given will be returned fails to look into the heart of *Homo sapiens*. We should be renamed *Homo horribilis* until the day we mature into a wise and virtuous species.

3450. Would the Germans who engaged in genocide during World War II have changed their behavior in response to kind and loving acts of captives?

Reform

3451. Lasting reform would be possible if each and every one of us realized that the welfare of all of humanity is in our self-interest.

Refusal

3452. Give no reason for a refusal, and it is not likely you will be asked again.

Regret

3453. Regrets are the scourge of old age. They serve no useful purpose and divert our attention away from the privilege of life.

3454. Regret for inaction is untouched by time.

3455. The regrets of history change nothing.

3456. When regrets outweigh our dreams, life is nowhere to be found.

Religion

3457. A born-again doubter and thinker is likely to embrace morality untouched by fear.

3458. A caring God in a cruel world is easily embraced by fear-driven belief.

3459. A country where religion is popular has not escaped its infancy.

3460. A finely tuned universe that favors our existence does not justify belief in a loving God interested in our welfare.

3461. A God distant and aloof is far more believable than one modeled after humanity.

3462. A God who requires mindless adoration is all too human.

3463. A loving God is a quantum leap beyond intelligent design.

3464. A moral God would surely favor those who are good with no expectation of reward to those who drop to their knees in pursuit of eternal bliss.

3465. Actions motivated by expectation of reward have only the appearance of virtue.

3466. An atheistic humanist reveals tolerance and goodness rarely seen in the devout.

3467. Are we devout when we follow God's example and do nothing when faced with profound evil or catastrophe?

3468. Ascribing morality to a first cause is more desperation than inspiration.

3469. Belief in God clearly stems from fear of death, fear of loss of loved ones, and fear of eternal oblivion. Such belief is understandable even if unwarranted. Some of us who cannot embrace religion wish it were true.

3470. Believers confuse a majority opinion with truth.

3471. Deathbed conversions seem the essence of "too little, too late."

3472. Divine intervention selects us over them.

3473. According to doctrine, an omnipotent and omniscient being who permits evil to abound is pure goodness.

3474. Doubt is the crux of life, whereas belief is the bulwark of religion. They are eternal foes.

3475. Education has failed when a society embraces religion, for belief has replaced thought.

3476. "Eternal" is a scary word
that prompts some to believe
in doctrines they once thought absurd
that now serve to relieve—
bringing peace though they aggrieve.

3477. Every religious sect sees the errors of its competitors, and they are all correct.

3478. Evil has no limits when done in God's name.

3479. Faith: belief that ignores all evidence to the contrary.

3480. Faith is evidence of fear.

3481. Faith seems fine when we have time
to drop to our knees and pray.
But real life so full of strife
finds science saves the day—
may be we've found our way.

3482. Few believers celebrate the death of a loved one destined for heaven.

3483. For many, religion is the drug of choice.

3484. For religious belief to perish, as Bertrand Russell hopes, truth must transcend fear.

3485. Gandhi claims that no one can live without religion. His notion of life and religion must be broadly defined.

3486. God explains the inexplicable.

3487. God's will allows one to kill on a grand scale.

3488. Gods who are servants of human desires are rejected by all who think.

3489. Hatred of atheists is an expression of fear.

3490. Honest heathens do abound,
Christians are yet to be found.

3491. If religion makes us virtuous, then virtue must be redefined.

3492. If religion were free of reward, it would be more credible.

3493. If there is a God who created us in his own image, then we are doomed.

3494. If there were a God, he would surely censure those who believe without question.

3495. If there were no possibility of salvation, would you believe in a kind and loving God?

3496. If you were to live forever in perfect health, would you believe in God?

3497. Concerns about increasing the population on a planet with finite resources are irrelevant to those who are going to heaven.

3498. Intelligence is the enemy of religion. None of the commandments encourage critical thought.

3499. Interpretation allows religion to justify nearly every action.

3500. Kindness found without a creed
is bound for hell—a bad seed.

3501. Leaders find religion more useful than truthful.

3502. Many deeds performed in the name of God reveal the immorality of religion.

3503. Millions find divine deliverance to be their drug of choice.

3504. Order is not God, and chance is not the devil.

3505. Our flawed nature is revealed in the gods we have created.

3506. Parents fail their children when they teach them to believe without question.

3507. Piety is the conversion of fear.

3508. Prayer is the equivalent of begging for a change in policy.

3509. Religion claims to be the source of morality while not mentioning its participation in war.

3510. Religion claims to be the source of morality while delivering eternal punishment to those who do not believe.

3511. Religion embraces a mindless heaven or torturous hell.

3512. Religion is a drug that makes us feel better as we sin.

3513. Religion is an understandable response to the harsh realities of life. It may succeed where truth fails.

3514. Religion is full of fear,
shuns the devil of doubt.
Believers face the voir dire,
declare they are devout—
pray they won't wash out.

3515. Religion is operationally defined by its practitioners.

3516. Religion, like other drugs, brings an uneasy happiness.

3517. Religion never fails to insult its God, whereas agnosticism celebrates the doubt that defines our thoughtful nature.

3518. Religion promises an eternity of worship.

3519. Religion requires that we sacrifice a fine intellect on the altar of belief, denying every salient argument opposing the existence of a personal God interested in our welfare. Only the desperate embrace the absurd.

3520. Religion's face is revealed in its followers.

3521. Religious belief is fully embraced and understood by the irrational mind.

3522. Religious education is an oxymoron.

3523. Religious education is confined to one school of thought.

3524. Religious fervor embraces war in the name of morality.

3525. Religious mysteries are said to be beyond our comprehension and to be absolutely true.

3526. Religion replete with answers
censures those who question why.
Belief consoles crushing grief
with salvation's warm reply—
none who believe will die.

3527. So long as religion plays a powerful role in human affairs, our evolution is in jeopardy.

3528. The atheist is one who believes that the inability to prove God's existence is proof of his nonexistence.

3529. The clergy are respected for spreading comfortable delusions when people are faced with death.

3530. The clergy may embrace evolution of life as God's way, while rejecting the evolution of their own minds.

3531. The currency of the clergy continues to climb in the face of priestly misconduct and holy wars.

3532. The devil's diary is unavailable, giving God an unfair advantage.

3533. The dignity that could be ours vanishes in the fear-driven desperation of religion.

3534. The faithful can embrace moral bigotry when salvation is the grand prize.

3535. The existence of life as we know it requires a set of favorable conditions that some insist are the result of a cosmic creator who mysteriously became a loving savior. Such desperation convinces no one who thinks.

3536. The God of war is active and well among theists.

3537. The God who gave us a mind appears to prefer that we remain blind.

3538. "The Good Book" is the ultimate misnomer.

3539. The Good Book's influence is evident in a very bad world.

3540. The heart of religion is the heart of fear.

3541. The insincerity of religious belief is manifest in the behavior of believers.

3542. The intellectual bondage that inevitably accompanies religious belief is particularly dangerous in those who hold positions of power.

3543. The light of religion shone brightest in the Dark Ages.

3544. The magic of religion is seen in the converting of the mysterious into a loving deity.

3545. The need to believe in God is simply that: a need.

3546. The notion of a space-time continuum in which the past, present, and future have the same reality is not inconsistent with the notion of an all-knowing God who sees the future as easily as the past.

3547. The notion that a kind and loving God has created a world of savagery is simply absurd.

3548. The power of untenable belief is indisputable.

3549. The promise of eternal life is a powerful incentive to believe what appears to be absurd and contrary to all human experience.

3550. The promises and threats of religion provide a weak foundation for human welfare.

3551. The religious claim morality as their own while carrying Bibles into battle.

3552. Theism: a perfect God creates imperfect humans and then punishes them with eternal damnation for his mistake.

3553. Theism and atheism are the twin towers of ignorance, for how can we possibly know?

3554. Theology is a subject without subject matter.

3555. "There are no atheists in foxholes" speaks to human frailty, not to the existence of God.

3556. There is no force in the world more deadly than a religious zealot.

3557. There is no reflection in genuflection, only fearful adherence to a creed.

3558. There is so much of humanity in God that religion finally can be seen as love of self.

3559. Those who genuflect reflect on the life to come.

3560. Those who only postulate the existence of a personal God have more integrity than those with erroneous proof. Unfortunately, this honesty has nothing to do with truth.

3561. Threats of eternal damnation have failed to improve our species. Perhaps it's time to preach a morality free of reward and punishment.

3562. Associating vice with atheism and virtue with theism is the bigotry of the devout.

3563. To be born-again into agnosticism is to grow up.

3564. To embrace religion is to deny our evolution into a thoughtful species more inclined to questions than answers.

3565. To embrace religion is to embrace despotism, where even thought subjects us to eternal damnation.

3566. Efforts to harmoniously integrate science and religion are a triumph of desire over reason.

3567. Knowing God's will usually means having divine authority to do as we please.

3568. Saying that there may be a first cause has nothing to do with religion.

3569. War and wealth continue to find a home in religion.

3570. We do not love what we fear.

Religion and Intelligence

3571. If religion were to encourage and praise intelligence, it would be acting against its own best interest.

Religion and Science

3572. If science becomes a religion, it commits itself to the narrow vision of a disciple.

3573. Morality is no more dependent on religion than it is on science.

3574. Religion is immersed in fearful rejection of our mortality, whereas science embraces endless cycles of birth and death.

3575. Religion promises eternal life, while science sees the mortality of everything from starfish to stars.

3576. Science flourishes by rejection of authority, while religion embraces a higher authority.

3577. Science is based on the shifting sands of discovery; religion is founded on the rigid tenets of belief.

3578. Science poses puzzling questions, while religion swells with incontrovertible answers.

3579. Science pushes religion to the brink, where death is waiting.

3580. So long as science fails to provide eternal life, it is no threat to religion.

3581. The clergy proudly hold on tight
to what they see as true,
while science sees reality
difficult to pursue,
must change its point of view.

3582. The religion of science, with its gospel of
uncertainty and bible of evidence, seeks
knowledge wherever it leads.

Remembrance

3583. I remember, I remember
friends who have passed away.
So sad to see eternity
reveal its awful sway;
lost love is here to stay.

Reputation

3584. The willingness to believe the worst puts any
reputation in jeopardy.

3585. Youth should be treated kindly, for it takes time
to learn the value of a good name.

Resolution

3586. Resolutions are best kept in silence.

Respect

3587. Respect demanded is respect denied.

3588. Praising ourselves smacks more of self-importance than of self-worth, whereas silence is full of possibility.

Responsibility

3589. Those who don't carry their own weight resent those who carry it for them.

Restaurant

3590. I have spent many hours writing in restaurants and by chance have observed the joys and exigencies of the human condition.

Retirement

3591. Retirement is welcomed by those who happily design their own enjoyment.

3592. Retirement should be a time of passionate pursuits unspoiled by monetary concerns.

3593. Those who are financially secure but *must* keep working often have no imagination.

Revenge

3594. There is no nobility in forgiving those who harm our
loved ones, nor is there peace in settling the score.

3595. Vengeance prompts virtue to embrace vice,
making a victim twice.

Reverie

3596. Reverie is thought detached from its origins; it
admits no particulars.

Revolution

3597. Revolution does an about-face
to find an unchanged human race.

3598. Revolution revolves about a new star of the same
galaxy.

3599. The failure of revolution is found in our
unchanging human nature.

Right and Wrong

3600. We speak of right and wrong as though
we know one from the other;
each right is someone else's wrong,
we may one day discover.

Risk

3601. The old who encourage the young to lead a risky
life have rarely practiced what they preach.

Role-Playing

3602. We are judged by how well we play a role. Who
are we really?

Romance

3603. Beauty attracts, but character sustains.

Sadness

3604. For me, the saddest moments in life come with
the loss of loved ones. This must be a universal
sentiment.

Salvation

3605. Salvation found in every creed
corrupts each step we take,
for doing "good" becomes a need
where heaven is at stake
and virtue is a fake.

3606. Some say salvation is a gift
bestowed on the devout.
God pardons every evil act
except the sin of doubt—
seems a peculiar route.

3607. Within Christendom, the gift of salvation is a gift
with strings attached.

Satiety

3608. There is poverty that comes with wealth, a satiety
that by stealth places the simplest joys out of
reach.

Satire

3609. Satire sees vice as daily bread,
food for thought when well read.

3610. Satire should sting with insight.

Satisfaction

3611. Satisfaction with life is more a matter of creativity
than circumstance.

Scandal

3612. Guilt is softened by another's plight;
let each new scandal bring us sleep tonight.

Science

3613. All of science ultimately ends in the assertions of
physics and the language of mathematics.

3614. An exact science is approximate at best.

3615. As science moves forward with new discoveries, the
notion of God retreats into what is yet mystery.

3616. Insofar as social science deals with human nature,
it is the hardest of sciences.

3617. Science applies reason to the cauldron of belief,
where only what is seen and measured survives.

3618. Science cannot save us from ourselves.

3619. Science does not assume the permanence or
uniformity of natural law. Principles emerge
from many observations and measurements that
serve to explain and predict. Science is purely
inductive and readily abandons any rule that fails
to account for observed phenomena.

3620. Science fiction has trouble keeping pace with science.

3621. Science has its own bigotry that finds everything
beyond its method irrelevant or absurd.

3622. Science rejects the powerful biases of belief
in pursuit of tentative truth. It subjects its
hypotheses to test after test in pursuit of whatever
it might find.

3623. The measurements of science are useful in dealing
with a mysterious world. Causality remains ever
in the shadows.

3624. The mystery: the mathematician creates an
abstract world of elegant beauty that becomes an
invaluable tool of scientific inquiry.

3625. The realization that science explodes with new
knowledge and applications without
comparable wisdom is cause for concern.

3626. When science cannot explain a phenomenon,
many invoke the supernatural.

Seascape

3627. The ocean's view from a great ship
seems flat as flat can be.
The many curves of life submit
to truth we cannot see.

Secrets

3628. A secret revealed to one is revealed to all.

3629. Scoundrels welcome secrets, but those with
character would rather not know.

Security

3630. A feeling of genuine security can be found only
where law is unnecessary.

Self

3631. Allowing others to say the final word about us
may be an expensive way to avoid the appearance
of vanity.

3632. Changing the self is challenge beyond compare;
nature and nurture have caught us in their snare.

3633. The self is to be loved, denied, pitied, defended,
deceived—but never known.

3634. To convincingly talk of oneself
is difficult indeed.
To compliment or censure self
is seen as vanity.

3635. We hide under layers of propriety, never quite
escaping the primal self.

3636. Those who encourage us to be free of the self
never fully explain what this means or how it is
achieved.

3637. Being true to oneself can be a commitment to treachery.

Self-Control

3638. Self-control defines the quality of our life far more than intelligence or circumstance.

3639. We have evolved with the ability to control the self, notwithstanding the wars that abound.

Self-Deception

3640. We often lie to ourselves with conviction that seals our fate.

Self-Denial

3641. Abstinence is desire's jailer.

3642. Self-denial is most willing to share its austerity.

Self-Esteem

3643. If your sense of worth depends on the opinion of others, however great, you are unworthy.

Self-Fulfillment

3644. Fulfilling oneself may seem unquestionably good
until we examine the nature of self and its goals.

Self-Image

3645. A positive self-image manages to set aside the
human nature we have come to know.

3646. A self-portrait untouched by truth is beautiful
indeed.

3647. Confidence and high self-esteem are traits
commonly found among tyrants.

3648. We call them animals with some disdain,
display great works of ego's endless train.
Our primate heritage lost in self-regard,
we would be angels—a pure canard.

Self-Interest

3649. Our biological uniqueness appears to have
universal themes, not the least of which is
self-interest.

3650. Physicians may not be averse
to illness that abounds.
Much wealth accrues before the hearse
makes its timely rounds.

3651. Elevating oneself by helping others is self-interest redeemed.

3652. We rarely do the right thing if it conflicts with some personal advantage. Self-interest is essentially amoral.

Self-Knowledge

3653. Few have courage to face the self,
alone and naked in the night,
stripped to the bone with second sight,
undone in unremitting light.

3654. Our life's work may serve us well enough,
while real talent lies dormant in the rough.

3655. Self-knowledge is rarely sought and often shunned.

Self-Love

3656. Self-love is seen admitting sin,
pure honesty without a spin.

Self-Pity

3657. Self-pity is perfectly understandable in those who experience misfortune on every front, but self-pity does not mean defeat and may inspire the courage to overcome.

Self-Portrait

3658. Call me a philosopher, one who finds questions in answers.

Self-Rejection

3659. Society would benefit greatly by self-rejection among those who do harm. Rejection of an evil self should not be discouraged.

3660. The act of judging oneself harshly is tainted with a hint of pride.

3661. To not believe in yourself is to announce to the world that you are unworthy.

Self-Reliance

3662. Self-reliance is a myth. Most of us rely on others in some way our entire life. This dependency is greater in childhood and old age.

Self-Respect

3663. A dog's admiration is not the best measure of one's worth.

3664. A higher power is not required for self-respect, nor is morality delivered to us by some God. We can value ourselves because we have decided to do what is right.

3665. Applause: self-respect should stand on firmer ground.

3666. If your self-respect is dependent on the encouragement of friends, it is too fragile for real-world exposure.

3667. Self-respect comes easily to those convinced the self is hidden—no one knows.

3668. Self-respect may require forgiveness on a grand scale.

3669. To be rich in self-respect is to be poor in virtue.

3670. Praising ourselves smacks more of self-importance than of self-worth, whereas silence is full of possibility.

Sentimentality

3671. The sentimental spread their tears
so thin that we wonder why.
They pretend to apprehend
deep sorrow's stern outcry
for loss that will not die.

SETI

3672. Are the visitors hunters
with intelligence to prevail,
travelers who plunder
every planet on their trail?
We send signals to the stars,
hoping for a warm reply,
while man's nasty alter ego
may appear in the sky.

3673. The UFO phenomenon has provoked millions to
wonder while many in the scientific community
have discreetly looked away.

3674. Upon first contact with an alien race, dare we tell
the truth?

3675. We announce our presence and location in the
Milky Way and expect alien visitors to be kind
and considerate and embrace our flawed race.

Sex

3676. There is a tyranny we wish to keep,
for when sex dies, we face eternal sleep.

Shakespeare

3677. Critics of Shakespeare's work show learning's place,
mere servants to the genius of the race.

3678. Shakespeare's total grasp of the universal comes to life in his many characters.

3679. The shadow of Shakespeare descends upon all who presume to write.

Shame

3680. Law is a guide, but shame is a command.

3681. Shame may be a measure of moral maturity or may merely be the superficiality of cultural bias.

3682. The absence of shame is the presence of evil.

3683. The blush of shame is virtue's proper hue.

3684. We can be ashamed of doing what many consider right.

3685. Without shame, there is no morality.

Silence

3686. If you see safety in silence, you have the wisdom to know what you don't know.

3687. Saying nothing allows the possibility of wisdom and avoids the certainty of error.

3688. Silence provokes thoughts of the great void that permeates all of existence.

3689. Silence requires the least effort for the most good.

3690. The stern disapproval of silence rings in our ears.

3691. Uncomfortable silence may bring uncomfortable thought.

Simplicity

3692. Simplifying may convert a complex reality into a simple falsehood.

Sin

3693. Abstinenece in old age is deprivation by default.

3694. Each of us sees sin as well-defined.

3695. Since behavior defines us, the notion of loving the sinner and hating the sin is manifestly absurd.

3696. To love a sinner is to love the sin, for they are one.

Sincerity

3697. Candor is the home of cruelty.

3698. Is it better to be sincerely mean
or conceal the impulse to be obscene?

3699. Sincerity can bring cruelty with the comfort of good conscience.

3700. Sincerity embraces the thorny heart of self, where truth is rarely kind.

3701. Sincerity is cherished most by those who have little to lose.

3702. Sincerity is effortless, whereas feigning is a burden no one can sustain.

3703. Sincerity lays human nature bare.

3704. The monsters among us are quite sincere.

3705. There is sincerity in the silence of dissent.

3706. To be sincere is to be true
to what is in our heart;
May be as sweet as a billet-doux
that speaks with timeless art
or bear dark words that smart.

3707. Bending truth in the service of kindness is sincerity of the heart.

3708. To embrace sincerity is to welcome our darkest thoughts as though they were friends.

3709. When alone, we gaze into a mirror that strips away the clothing of our thought.

Size

3710. A cloud that eclipses the sun puts size in
perspective.

Slander

3711. Liars can do us in with a finesse
that truth can never match with pure noblesse.

3712. Slander lives through the audience that sustains it.

3713. To never endure the sting of ill will,
remain unknown without a trace of skill.

Sleep

3714. Sleep, that realm of mysterious unrest,
releases demons of the day and more.
Yearns for truth yet hides from the quest,
in the language of dreams at truth's back door.

Small Things

3715. After reading a few aphorisms, a friend of a
friend who was a well-known scientist suggested
I write a book. This offhand remark prompted
the writing of several books. Perhaps there are no
small things.

3716. There are mathematical formulations and brief poems that rival tomes of one thousand pages.

Smiles

3717. Smiles seduce with friendly guile,
true feelings hidden, still on trial.
Look deeply, far beyond the grin;
you may find joy or maybe sin.

3718. Smiles: the heart's fugitive feelings that devastate and delight.

Smoker

3719. The fiery tube lights up a sad grimace,
chained to the smoke that darkens all his space.

Snow

3720. The falling snow might be a blessing if it were not for a government threatening punishment for not shoveling the walks.

Society

3721. No society can endure without adopting kindness as its first principle.

3722. Presidential awards are not given to those who strive to improve society by challenging those in power.

3723. The madness of nations is found in patriotic pride.

3724. The unrestricted legality of parenthood ensures societal chaos.

3725. Those honored by society when they are alive are not likely to be nonconformists.

Soldiers

3726. A soldier who follows orders without question renounces his humanity.

3727. Soldiers who think on their feet may walk away from war.

3728. Soldiers are not encouraged to be citizens, for citizens are obliged to question every decision of the government.

3729. The most effective soldiers hold patriotism above morality.

Solitude

3730. Solitude fosters poetry and philosophy, which thrive in the serene atmosphere of remembrance.

3731. Solitude is wonderful and true
so long as one dear friend is there for you.

3732. Solitude prompts imagination to reign, with no
limit to joy or pain.

3733. The companions of solitude are thoughts.

3734. The society of solitude is inescapable, and we are
most alone in a crowd.

3735. What we call solitude is replete with what we
cannot forget. We are never alone while alive.

Song

3736. My songs stretch from the momentary to the
eternal, with wonder and a search for meaning.

Sorrow

3737. A tear is the lens of sorrow.

3738. If there is pleasure in sorrow, there was no love.

3739. Our life rests on a foundation of inescapable
sorrow that gives every living moment meaning.

3740. Sorrow brings a childlike honesty devoid of
pretense.

3741. Sorrow brings us all to the common ground of
desolation, where no differences endure.

3742. Sorrow is the stuff of life,
for when loved ones die,
the real is all we can feel—
grief cannot lie.

3743. Sorrow unites us in common despair, from which those who love the most never escape.

3744. Sorrows are with us for life. No therapy can sweep them away.

3745. The greater the joy, the more profound the sorrow.

3746. There are memories that bring fresh tears of sorrow as though time stood still.

Soul

3747. Every time the word *soul* is used, I become more confused.

3748. The scientist who speaks of the soul has become a theologian.

3749. The soul appears to be the nonentity we cherish most when faced with our oblivion.

3750. The soul is surrounded by words that attempt to conceal its nonexistence.

3751. The writer who speaks of an immortal soul and eternal life has found an audience.

3752. Applying the notions of science to the soul is equivalent to saying that religious doctrine is fundamental to scientific thought.

3753. Postulating the existence of the soul is an act of desperation in a species that should know better.

3754. To speak of a soul is to confuse a symbol with reality. In pursuit of immortality, we create worlds of nonsense.

Space Travel

3755. If space travel is too expensive, then so is life, for our very survival depends on escaping Mother Earth.

Specialist

3756. The specialist who ignores philosophy is blind to fundamental truth.

3757. Thoughtful immersion in the particular is a kind of thoughtlessness.

Speech

3758. Eyes and ears appear so wise,
    but speech affords no disguise.

3759. Speech is best when we realize
much that we say is our surmise;
doubt is the bedrock of the wise.

3760. Saying nothing allows wisdom to fill the air.

3761. To think profoundly before speaking is rare indeed.

3762. We say the kindest words and then
add insult to the brew.
We wonder if we'll ever be
one who is always true.

3763. We speak our mind and often find we've crossed
the line.

Spontaneity

3764. How dreadful to allow spontaneity to reveal the
uncensored self.

Statistics

3765. Statistics is mathematics that gives license to logic.

Status

3766. So long as wealth and position confer societal
status and simple virtue is ignored, our future is
in jeopardy.

Striving

3767. Striving is best when we have some ability to perform.

3768. We stumble on our way to perfection beyond our grasp.

Struggle

3769. The struggle of my retirement has been to write a significant book.

3770. There is no struggle to love; it is as natural as breath.

Student

3771. The best students are devoted to the subject, with little thought of preparing for exams.

Stupidity

3772. Many governments cherish the stupidity that fosters unquestioning acceptance.

3773. Stupidity has an advantage over intelligence by way of limitations. No mouse ever created an atomic bomb.

Success and Failure

3774. If you rely on others to define your success, you have failed.

3775. Living in a great mansion is failure on display.

3776. Our failure defines our success.

3777. Success has so many personas, one wonders how it should be defined.

3778. Success may be the attainment of ignoble goals, and failure may valiantly pursue the good. Which would you applaud?

3779. Taking the long view puts success and failure in perspective; to strive is to thrive.

3780. The thought of success continues to sustain those who have failed.

3781. Those who see tragedy in success have chosen the wrong path.

3782. Failing in a great cause is a kind of success.

3783. Satisfying your dreams can be a failure of sorts.

3784. We speak of success and failure as though there is a commonly accepted set of values.

3785. When success is measured in dollars and cents, right and wrong are left on the fence.

Suggestions

3786. Suggestions well-received are preconceived.

Suicide

3787. If your only purpose is death, you are not alive.

Sunday

3788. Some go to church on Sunday morn
for faith and things to come;
I sit and write of things forlorn
with thoughts that make me numb—
of when we must succumb.

Superiority

3789. The presumption of superiority is not likely to
bring love and beauty into the world.

3790. When members of a race claim genetic
superiority, they prove they have none.

Supernatural

3791. Those who see the supernatural in every event are
more in touch with need than with reality.

Supreme Court
•
3792. The Supreme Court has found its way,
with God the only guide.
The law bends to religion's sway
with church and state allied.

Surveillance

3793. With cameras found on every street,
Orwell's world has come to life.
Be careful who by chance you meet;
Big Brother's eye is indiscreet.

Switzerland

3794. Perhaps we should all follow the Swiss path to
"ignoble" peace.

3795. The behavior of the Swiss should not be ignored
in pursuit of national self-interest.

3796. The neutrality of the Swiss may seem heartless,
until we see the thousands killed in pursuit of
unattainable justice and peace.

3797. The Swiss are happily ignored by the many
warring nations.

3798. The Swiss have threatened no one and have
managed to live in peace and prosperity.

3799. The United States may learn something from a country that has chosen to profit more from watches than from weapons.

3800. We should applaud the Swiss for not searching the world for supposedly just wars.

Taboo

3801. Taboos are the safety net of society.

Tact

3802. Tact makes a point without putting one out of joint.

3803. Tact's point rarely disappoints.

3804. The tactful read our feelings and ignore our words.

Talent

3805. One should not confuse talent with fame.

3806. Talents abound, though desire and circumstance may prevent their development or recognition.

3807. Those with little talent give little praise.

3808. We pay homage to those born with a gift and ignore many who put all into what they are.

Taste

3809. Current taste can call great artistic achievement rubbish.

Taxes

3810. There is no substantive difference between robbing a dead man on the street and the death tax.

3811. Those who know the least about income tax pay the most.

Teacher

3812. A bad example is a good teacher.

3813. A teacher should feel compelled to teach.

3814. The best teachers inspire more questions than answers.

3815. The teacher must be careful not to inhibit students' natural desire to learn.

Teaching

3816. Teaching reveals that you do not know what you thought you knew.

3817. The best teaching is done by those who struggle with their subject. To be gifted is to dismiss the many steps required by lesser minds.

3818. Those who teach never fail to teach themselves.

3819. To teach well, let your own experience invade the subject taught.

Tears

3820. Love sees clearly through the blurred vision of tears.

3821. Tears shed for another's pain reveal humanity yet humane.

3822. Tears wash away the lies.

3823. Though many years have passed, there are events that bring forth tears. Time erases everything but love.

3824. We are exposed by what brings us to tears.

Technology

3825. Technical skill is more manipulation than understanding.

3826. Technology has armed the dominant predator of planet Earth with new teeth.

3827. Technology, which was thought to be our savior, has put thousands out of work.

3828. Technology brings, in increasing order of importance, comfort, convenience, and jeopardy.

3829. The creation of nuclear weapons provokes one to question the survival value of intelligence.

3830. The many whose best performance is mediocre are competing with machines, and the machines are winning.

3831. The technology we cherish, when applied to war, may bring us to extinction.

Temperance

3832. The best of health is assured
with temperance our guide;
the problem to be cured
must face the devil Hyde,
who lingers deep inside.

Testament

3833. Wills should be well-defined, or lawyers will be next in line.

Things

3834. To love things is to miss the point of life.

Thought

3835. A book of thoughts that fails to offend is without merit.

3836. An abstraction is easily embraced, but the real is full of unexpected contingencies.

3837. An implied question mark ends every profound thought.

3838. Having an open mind has come to mean accepting any new idea because it is new.

3839. Deep thought is dangerous, for the cherished beliefs that sustain us may vanish in deliberations not to be ignored.

3840. For many, hopes and fears are the vehicles of thought, and unsympathetic reason is cast aside.

3841. Great intellect entertains all thoughts and embraces none.

3842. In an attempt to escape the physical, some say that thought is independent of the brain that gave it birth. We yearn for immortality.

3843. It is difficult to find fault with science when it is certain only that it is uncertain.

3844. It is easy to say that narrow minds make broad statements, but so do philosophers and mathematicians.

3845. We may never see the essence
of what is in plain view;
our mind has soared and explored
before we bid adieu.

3846. Our opinions are precious because they are personal, not because they are true.

3847. Our thoughts are a self-portrait we cannot deny.

3848. Proof follows an intuitive leap.

3849. Russell claims we fear thought; perhaps the cherished beliefs that sustain us must never be challenged.

3850. The deepest thought finds its way
to doubt all that people say,
for the world we've come to know
may be no more than vertigo.

3851. The life span of an idea is often more dependent on utility than on truth.

3852. The moment we are convinced, we are lost.

3853. The stronger an opinion, the weaker the thought.

3854. The thinker is one who rejects the followership so prized by society.

3855. The will to believe expresses the desire to remain ignorant.

3856. The writer hopes that his passionate pursuit of thought will serve to inspire those who may someday look his way.

3857. There is no difference between those who do not think at all and those who consult some higher authority to discover their point of view.

3858. Though we cannot escape the thoughts of others, we strive to leave a trail of our own.

3859. Thought born of fear or desire is likely to be false.

3860. Our thoughts define *our* world, not *the* world.

3861. Thought should be entertained, not ordained.

3862. Thoughts range in beauty, as they do in truth.

3863. Thought that brings accurate predictions is useful and can be false.

3864. Thought's unpopularity is founded on its freedom, which puts all established doctrine in jeopardy.

3865. To be thoughtful is to challenge cherished belief.

3866. To embrace uncertainty without dismay is to think.

3867. Exploring the obvious is beyond subtlety.

3868. We can only hope that many thoughts never come to fruition.

3869. We provoke thought when we rupture the cherished balloons of belief.

3870. What is thought to be clarity rests on the murky substratum of unanswered questions.

3871. When conviction arises from fear, fiction appears.

3872. When thinking for yourself is disastrous, it is time for a consultation.

3873. When we say, "It is a matter of opinion," we are often attempting to legitimize the absurd.

3874. Where time is money, deep thought is nonexistent.

Thrift

3875. Some say live within your means
and fulfill your precious dreams;
this seems very fine advice
till all you eat is rancid rice.

Time

3876. As long as you have thoughts to explore, no one can steal your irreplaceable time.

3877. Our faith in the future, however unwarranted,
      makes the present tolerable.

3878. The only time travel possible at the moment is
      influencing the future by learning from the past.

3879. The past did its best to teach,
      but passions do run deep.
      We knew our way would betray
      the wisdom that time reaps.
      Our missteps play for keeps.

3880. The present is all we have; embrace it with love,
      for the past is gone and the future will inevitably
      end badly.

3881. The present is all we have. The past and the
      future are bleak eternities.

3882. There are times when time becomes the
      centerpiece of life.

3883. Time is the eternal river
      we travel for a spell.
      Thrust between eternities,
      we feel each sad farewell;
      seems life's a bagatelle.

3884. Time's arguments are irrefutable.

3885. Recognizing the value of time is the first step in
      using it wisely.

3886. Watching time pass is simply intolerable.

3887. We hope to buy time by conforming to the doctor's rules.

3888. We measure our lives by the movements of celestial bodies approaching an eternity beyond our grasp.

3889. We reveal who or what we love through our use of time; it is the stuff of life.

Tolerance

3890. For tolerance to be justified, it must pass through the sieve of morality.

3891. In a world of moral relativity, tolerance knows no limits.

3892. Once tolerance is a habit, all is lost.

3893. Our tolerance of someone or something is more dependent on the relationship than on reality.

3894. Those who find tolerance intolerable have convictions.

3895. To tolerate what's clearly wrong
is evil to the core;
intolerance is to be strong
when others bow before
conventions we deplore.

3896. We are open to everything when we are closed to nothing.

3897. When we tolerate pure evil, we are revealing our indifference to morality.

Totalitarianism

3898. Dictatorship has an efficiency that freedom will not permit.

3899. To silence someone is to turn him or her against you.

Tradition

3900. Our love of tradition has continued to be expressed in war.

3901. The dead live on in respect for tradition, for better or worse.

3902. There is no fundamental challenge to tradition. Human nature prevails.

3903. Those who do not stop and think find tradition to be more than a guide.

Tragedy

3904. Tragedy is now heard round the world; no one escapes its haunting echoes.

Training

3905. Training defines us by limiting our powers of observation. We see what we are programmed to see.

Travel

3906. Ancient and modern Egypt, with its pyramids and skyscrapers, Coptic Christians, and Muslims, no longer welcomes those who returned year after year with enthusiasm untouched by ennui.

3907. I have traveled with the English often and have found that the language is still theirs.

3908. Traveling well involves not merely changing your view, but changing your point of view.

3909. Travel at its best
puts bias to rest.

3910. Travel may expand one's horizons, but changing the scene may not change the self.

3911. We see home in a new light when we travel the world.

Trifle

3912. Take care what you trifles call,
for all there is arose from small
unlikely places like the speck,
expanding ever as we trek
on a globe that makes us wonder,
are we nothing blown asunder?

Triviality

3913. What appears trivial at the moment may become
the most momentous event in our life. We simply
don't know.

3914. What is trivial to one is a life-altering insight to
another.

Trust

3915. To believe that trust begets trust is to have little
experience and much hope.

3916. Trusting nobody must include oneself.

3917. Trust is sometimes warranted, but mistrust is ever
woebegone.

Truth

3918. A healing lie is truth that matters.

3919. A writer tries to write the truth
and finds his face in every proof.

3920. Absolute truth is a fiction embraced by the clergy
and abandoned by modern science.

3921. Answers are impediments to truth. There is
always more to say.

3922. Atoms and molecules whirl about truth,
exclaiming, "Catch me if you can."

3923. Belief finds its way to great joy
while truth descends to destroy.

3924. Clarity is seductive and can be mistaken for truth.

3925. Clichés represent consensus that may be true.

3926. Conflicting points of view
are as good as true
when we have no clue.

3927. Convictions strangle what passes for truth into
submission.

3928. Distance lends not only enchantment but also
insight.

3929. Error is often a glittery flaw,
but truth lies deep in fundamental law.

3930. Even an unknown writer is hesitant to speak the truth.

3931. Even fact has a way of capitulating to bias.

3932. Facts, filtered as they are through biological systems, only seem to have that well-defined solidity that leads to truth.

3933. Fairness to both sides misleads when only one side has merit.

3934. Fundamental questions rarely find definitive answers.

3935. Generalization: our desires transform a scintilla of evidence into a universe of self-deception we call truth.

3936. If you wish to know the price of truth, reveal your uncensored thoughts.

3937. If you wish to offend, truth is a better weapon than lies.

3938. Illusion sustains, but truth ordains.

3939. In a world fraught with perils, few welcome uncompromising truth.

3940. In pursuit of truth, we search for the essential and find ourselves.

3941. In the pursuit of truth, reverence for greatness is deadly.

3942. It is difficult to love truth, since it may go against everything we desire or believe.

3943. It is presumptuous to reject chaos because we need order.

3944. It is presumptuous to suppose that what we see as natural law is immutable.

3945. It is true that denying truth can bring comfort.

3946. Life is meaningful and meaningless. Polar opposites can both be true.

3947. Look for the exceptions that permeate much of what we call truth.

3948. Most prefer the lies of humility to the truth of a boast. Integrity has its limits.

3949. Much of what we call truth is tied to the tether of belief, where hope and fear create the world.

3950. No thinking person believes his or her opinions are absolutely true.

3951. One wonders why we seek the truth,
for joy is seldom found.
The mind will find convincing proof
of life's dark battleground.

3952. Only a brute can stand before truth with no tears.

3953. Our commitment to truth would be tested by censuring those who admire us, for fault can always be found.

3954. Our enemies speak a truth that our friends find unspeakable.

3955. Perception and language vie for dominance in the pursuit of truth.

3956. Provocative lies can inspire a search for truth.

3957. Scientific instruments used to "see" the world are subject to the way we think. There is no way to escape our biology in pursuit of truth.

3958. Should we admire Adolf Hitler for being true to himself?

3959. Few have been popular while telling truth.

3960. Some truth lies dormant in the safety zone of silence, where escape is too horrible to imagine.

3961. Speak the truth and let the profit go,
for those who seek to please reap as they sow.

3962. The agnostic's assertion of ignorance is more rational than real.

3963. The appearance of bias makes some reluctant to speak the truth.

3964. The approximations of integral calculus bring us truth with acceptable error. Absolute truth is a will-o'-the wisp.

3965. The closer we come to truth, the more we're inclined to laugh or cry.

3966. The cosmic perspective consigns all to oblivion.

3967. A diagnosis of impending death makes the notion that truth is beauty patently absurd.

3968. The discovery of error is a kind of truth.

3969. The explanation of some event may not be explainable in terms of what is already known. Occam's razor is a useful principle, but the world may be far more complex and subtle than we can imagine.

3970. The polar opposites that dominate our thinking have little to do with the infinite gradations that must characterize that mysterious realm called reality.

3971. The possession of truth titillates, but the use of truth can weigh heavily on one's conscience.

3972. The pursuit of comfort discourages the pursuit of truth.

3973. The search for truth is the cause of much discord.

3974. The truth is full of jeopardy
in childhood and beyond.
We learn to lie and satisfy
when we must respond—
the only way to bond.

3975. The truth we face is confronted with a multitude of untenable beliefs that manage to sustain multitudes.

3976. The unqualified is rarely true.

3977. There are truths one dare not express even in old age.

3978. There are truths that rarely make a public appearance; discreet lies are far more palatable.

3979. There is seldom a reverence for truth, for what we desire often becomes the bulwark of belief.

3980. Those who favor truth without restraint will feel its sting without complaint.

3981. Those of us who claim to speak the truth are more involved with pursuit than possession.

3982. Those who destroy with honesty defend themselves by saying, "I was only telling the truth."

3983. Those who hold an opinion in the face of overwhelming evidence to the contrary have found the world they wish to inhabit. Perhaps they know best.

3984. Those who say there are no new truths have never studied science.

3985. Those who worship truth ignore its consequences.

3986. To be true to yourself may be a commitment to profound evil.

3987. To pursue truth is to begin by rejecting much of what we wish were true.

3988. To say that truth is beautiful is to embrace
the indifference of nature and the dark side of
humankind.

3989. To say we must love truth is to embrace every evil
deed and catastrophe as a blessing.
No one who thinks expects truth to bring joy.

3990. Seeing deeply is more than we can bear;
truth taken in small portions is all we dare.

3991. "See things as they are" is easy to say and difficult
to do. This approach is reserved for those whose
goal is the unbiased pursuit of truth.

3992. To seek truth is not to love truth. We look
because we must.

3993. Truth doesn't care what we think or how we feel.

3994. Truth is not beautiful; it merely is.

3995. Truth is snail-paced, whereas falsehood wins the
race.

3996. Truth is stranger than fiction because it is not
limited by human imagination.

3997. Truth is useful insofar as it can explain and
predict.

3998. Truth knows nothing of kindness, for it has no
ulterior motives.

3999. Truth may not survive a passion for fairness.

4000. Truth often finds the labyrinth of needs, desires, and fears impassable.

4001. Truth remains as remote as mathematical formulation until branded with the fiery prod of experience.

4002. Truth rests on the shaky foundation of doubt, where the fragile hypothesis is revised continuously.

4003. Truth's tenure is brief at best, each fallen axiom will attest.

4004. Truth that is twisted ever so slightly is the greatest source of error.

4005. Truth, unlike belief, is easily rejected, for it rarely performs miracles.

4006. Truth revealed to revile puts the human race on trial.

4007. We are admonished to love truth, which reveals that all we hold dear ultimately vanishes.

4008. We are ultimately confronted with truth that saddens and falsehood that gladdens.

4009. We seek truth in elegant attire and find bits and pieces in the mire.

4010. What is true is rarely embraced when it conflicts with what we must believe.

4011. What we call truth is often belief in fear's clothing.

4012. What we call truth is often no more than the consensual validation of the moment.

4013. When danger provokes belief, the only truth to be seen is fear.

4014. When speaking the truth, it is best to have an escape plan.

4015. When there is no dissenting opinion—beware!

4016. When we challenge beliefs that bring us comfort, we show our commitment to truth.

Truth and Lies

4017. A physician has failed who will not, on occasion, deliver an inaccurate diagnosis.

4018. A truth designed to give us pain
is worse than lies of any strain.

4019. A truth that's told to bring us down
is worse than lies can be,
for in the end none can defend
against such treachery—
what hellish honesty.

4020. The demand for truth is tempered by its consequences.

4021. The pain that simple truth can bring
is more than lies can know,
for conscience can forever cling
to shame that will not go.

4022. Those who proudly stand upright
with truth their only guide
are blind to the tender light
of those who've loved and lied—
true goodness without pride.

Tyranny

4023. Tyranny enslaves both tyrant and subject.

4024. Tyranny will take hold wherever mindless
conformity is a willing accomplice.

4025. Tyrants do not act alone; they are sustained by
multitudes.

Uncertainty

4026. Facts are accumulations,
data found in what we see;
truth is deliberation
steeped in uncertainty.

Understanding

4027. It is not impossible to hate those we understand.

4028. Stepping into another's shoes
may bring understanding
that many, many Auschwitz Jews
would simply find damning.

4029. The limits of our understanding are clear to those
who ask fundamental questions.

4030. To understand the monsters among us is not to
forgive them.

Unhappiness

4031. Unhappiness is no stranger in paradise.

Useful

4032. Beauty is useful when it brings us joy.

4033. Belief can be useful though it be false.

4034. There is nothing more useful than love.

Utility

4035. Utility is a dangerous master, for the morality of means becomes irrelevant.

Utopia

4036. The human mind conceives of a utopia that human nature can never experience.

Vanity

4037. Better vanity in pursuit of virtue than evil without a hint of pride.

4038. Considering the oblivion that confronts us all, vanity is simply absurd.

4039. The weak foundation of vanity can be seen in a need for praise.

4040. There is no greater vanity than to see ourselves as deserving of salvation.

4041. Vanity can be seen in the silence of those who fear appearing foolish.

4042. Who can be vain walking through a cemetery?

4043. Would we be capable of vanity if we were privy to those whispers behind closed doors?

Variety

4044. Love wants no variety; it has found what it needs.

Vice

4045. Vice of a moderate sort
    makes life worth living;
    a little mischief helps to thwart
    serious sinning.

4046. When we love, we embrace vice, for no one is perfect.

Violence

4047. Evil abounds, and killing is done
    over and over, till no one has won.

Virtue

4048. The many "just" wars provide ample evidence that virtue is not well-defined.

4049. The notion that kindness given will inevitably be returned is one we are reluctant to abandon in spite of overwhelming evidence to the contrary.

4050. The "thou shall not" approach to morality sees virtue as abstinence without a single act of kindness.

4051. Virtue is rarely pure,
untouched by any sinning.
Virtue is demure
but not averse to winning.

4052. Virtue has become part of nature with the appearance of humanity.

4053. Virtue to some is a performing art.

4054. We on occasion may regret our virtue, until we consider the dire consequences of vice.

Virtue and Vice

4055. If vice finds virtue a useful tool, is it still virtue?

4056. Our vices are often endearing, whereas our virtues can be seen as censure.

4057. Theism can be immoral, and atheism can be deeply virtuous.

4058. Those who merely do no harm are life's dropouts. Do the dead deserve our respect because they are without vice?

4059. Too much virtue finds itself in a straitjacket of propriety, devoid of life.

4060. Vice seems more contagious than virtue.

4061. Virtue and vice are servants of self-interest.

Volunteer

4062. To volunteer without pay is to deprive someone of work.

Walking

4063. Walking works the body and mind. I think and write as I walk.

Wants

4064. To want less is to have more.

War

4065. A country in search of tyrants to topple will be ever at war.

4066. A country that allows an influential few to profit from war is immoral.

4067. A country that employs mercenaries in war has lost the support of its citizens.

4068. A country that engages in preemptive war has learned nothing from history.

4069. A country that rejects war while thousands of innocents die is embracing Christian values. Where do you stand, with Christ or against him?

4070. A country that searches the world for just wars is not peaceful.

4071. A prisoner of war
is a killer who has failed;
we are asked to treat him well
so he may yet prevail.

4072. A soldier follows orders to a tee,
no conscience on the road to victory;
God and country, hungry for a win,
set aside sacred oaths without sin.

4073. A well-educated citizenry would put war in jeopardy.

4074. America follows a long tradition of encouraging the poor to die for the rich.

4075. Armed conflict is said to keep us safe;
enemies are at the door,
phantoms that those in power
use to encourage war.

4076. Blood spills in pursuit
of justice on both sides,
all following the route
to victory denied.

4077. Citizen-soldiers who do not question their country's declaration of war become complicit in all that follows.

4078. Courage is not found in guns galore.
Manhood is built on peace, not war.

4079. So-called courageous leaders who wish to start a war hide behind the word "preemptive" in an attempt to justify the inevitable depravity that follows.

4080. Every war is justified by allusions to "necessity."

4081. Fighting a country's imprudent war falls short of heroism.

4082. How many leaders lose the respect of all thinking people by allowing thousands to die in war to save face or to look strong?

4083. Human groups are essentially alike, making the killing simply absurd.

4084. Ideals are the ammunition we use to load our guns.

4085. If the popularity of war is based on a thrill-seeking escape from boredom, then the human race is merely despicable.

4086. In defense of war, peace at *any* price may be peace at too great a cost.

4087. In the United States, when corporate sponsors encourage war for profit, there is little chance for peace.

4088. In war, fathers outlive their sons, and vice outlives virtue.

4089. In war, we speak of rules of engagement as though it is an athletic event.

4090. It is no surprise to see soldiers come to know that pointless killings accomplish nothing. Many take their own life rather than prolong the madness.

4091. It is true that tyranny brings peace at too great a cost.

4092. Last place in pursuit of war deserves all the accolades.

4093. Leaders of most countries favor indoctrination over education when it comes to war.

4094. National honor cries out,
"We must win!"
We finally withdraw,
no admission of sin.

4095. No matter how justified
the bloody war may be,
shame should be the name we give
to every victory.

4096. No one is told
nothing will change,
for war never ends.
'Tis the law of the range.

4097. Old men are big on war—
      must get even and do right.
      No cost is too great,
      say these sages out of sight.
      From the comfort of their chairs,
      they put humanity in crosshairs.

4098. One wonders whether the intelligence used to kill
      thousands will one day find the wisdom to seek
      peace.

4099. Our human nature makes preparation for war a
      dangerous business.

4100. Our superiority to all other life vanishes in the
      wounds of war.

4101. Over and over
      we cry, "We must win!"
      Humanity defeated
      by war's mortal sin.

4102. Preventive war is inventive war. We find the best
      reasons to do our worst.

4103. Preventive war: no one is fooled by those who
      strike first, claiming self-defense.

4104. Self-defense is so broadly defined that war is
      inevitable.

4105. Self-esteem is very fine
      when kindness is the goal,
      but killing well is a hell
      that no one should extol.

4106. So long as followers abound, there are those who will find their way to war.

4107. So long as killing is honored and those who refuse to fight are maligned, we will continue to wage war.

4108. So long as the human race insists on the "right to bear arms," its fate is assured.

4109. So long as the powerful find war profitable, it will occur.

4110. So long as we talk of honor and glory in war, we are doomed.

4111. The endless wars we fight for right
prove futile in the dead of night,
when the darkness lights the way
to killing well as we pray.

4112. The exclusivity of brotherhood makes war inevitable.

4113. The impulse to prevail, which is so evident in sports, may explain why many are more comfortable with war than with peace.

4114. The leader who wages war should not be immune to its consequences.

4115. The many die at twenty-two
to fill the coffers of the few.

4116. The notion that there is one true faith ensures the continuation of war.

4117. The old man's declaration of war should be met with the young man's declaration of peace.

4118. The only defense against nuclear fission is racial, religious, and national fusion.

4119. The prosperity of peace is the best answer to those who favor war.

4120. The real heroes are those who refuse to fight unjust wars.

4121. The religious warrior is more likely to wage nuclear war, for his rewards lie in the afterlife.

4122. The strongest nations look around
for ways to show their might,
so they wage war and God adore
when killing through the night,
savior on every site.

4123. The strongest nations create a bogus threat to justify their military adventurism.

4124. There is no Nobel Prize for war.

4125. Those democratic leaders who wage war should be asked whether they will encourage their offspring to sign up.

4126. Those who oppose war are never given a medal of honor.

4127. Those who speak of winning a war are incapable of preserving the peace.

4128. Interfering in the affairs of other countries is not a prescription for peace.

4129. Preparing for war encourages war. No one speaks of preparing for peace.

4130. To progress in the art of war is to regress in the art of living.

4131. To reject our dark nature
or the call of country pride
is to finally nurture
the goodness deep inside.

4132. To search the world for a just cause
seems goodness to the core;
but then we see morality
a mask for love of war;
we kill and God adore.

4133. Sending our citizens to war is a killing of sorts.

4134. The idea of waging war against war is not entirely without merit.

4135. To win a war is to create generations of enemies.

4136. War is a crime that has persisted for centuries and is now thought to be necessary or even virtuous.

4137. War is capitalism's answer to a recession.

4138. War is more a matter of followers than leaders.

4139. War is never good, but peace under tyranny is no better.

4140. War is often murder wrapped in national pride—
with God on our side.

4141. War is righteous homicide that rarely turns the
tide.

4142. War: a preferred method of problem solving
among *Homo sapiens.*

4143. War: how many must we kill to get even?

4144. We are a flawed race where tyrants abound. Each
country must find its own way to peace and
freedom.

4145. We are outraged by cruelty to animals, but we
embrace war.

4146. We are prone to use the skills we master.

4147. We made God our accomplice
in misdeeds of all kinds;
we sanctify sin
in defense of our crimes.

4148. We must support our troops' *unwillingness* to
fight preemptive war.

4149. We prepare for war with a diligence rarely found
in the pursuit of peace.

4150. We see war as a normal human endeavor, where
we create rules of engagement, lest we exceed the
bounds of propriety.

4151. We wage war to get even and find that the mathematics of war has no equality.

4152. When invading foreign lands,
nations cry self-defense.
Invading armies take the lands,
no matter what the evidence.

4153. When it is your profession to kill,
the heinous act is honed to a skill.

4154. When we withdraw from war, we have won a battle with human nature.

4155. Wouldn't it be wonderful if the leaders who start wars were abandoned by those who fight wars?

Weakness

4156. The weak who survive on grit alone seem to have the greatest strength.

Wealth

4157. Dying rich leaves a legacy of greed and jealousy.

4158. Great wealth is found in desiring exactly what we possess.

4159. It is said that more wealth brings less religion, yet we all face mortality. Perhaps this abandonment of religion comes from some other place.

4160. Poor health reveals the limitations of wealth.

4161. Poor health teaches wealth that the part is not the whole.

4162. Real wealth can be measured by how many healthy breaths we take.

4163. The gravity of wealth attracts sycophancy.

4164. The philanthropy of old age proudly announces its legacy.

4165. The wealthy reveal their priorities when they build a garage larger than most homes.

4166. We all suppose if we were rich,
we would not act the way they do,
but power turns on a switch
that strips away all but the true.

4167. Wealth attracts beauty and finds avarice.

4168. Wealth breeds a dependency not far from poverty.

4169. Wealth cannot prevent despair or enhance joy;
but it may, through luxury, promote disease and quicken death.

4170. Wealth encourages good and evil to realize their full potential.

4171. Wealth is *kept* when given away.

4172. Wealth's conspicuous expenditures are monuments to a pointless life.

4173. Without money, everything fades into the
background of need—even love.

4174. Your wealth is defined by what you will not sell.

Weather

4175. No matter what the weather,
we look for change quite soon.
We can imagine something better,
though it be Brigadoon.

4176. The weather we complain about may be more
within than without.

Why

4177. "Why" is the one question that defies ultimate
answers. Why is there a universe?

4178. "Why" should not be asked when fundamental
issues such as existence, universes, or life are
discussed, for the answers given define our nature,
not the world at large.

Will

4179. Some seem good by nature without the need to
decide.

4180. We can take all those steps necessary for success and still fail.

Winning

4181. A catastrophic universe makes winning seem quite pointless.

4182. Winner of *what* is the question.

4183. Winning implies a finality that is unjustified.

4184. Winning is such a precious thing
in many games we play.
Olympians spend years to win
laurels that simply say,
"I was the best today."

Wisdom

4185. An aphorism is a brief statement of truth or sentiment, remembering that truth is a moving target.

4186. Brilliant humans discovered a secret of the tiny atom, which created the potential for death on a planetary scale. Bacon was right: "knowledge is power." And for the human race, wisdom remains ever elusive.

4187. Even those who attain self-knowledge find wisdom a distant prospect.

4188. It may be wise to believe the palpably false, for truth is without mercy.

4189. It is wise to see fortune as the final arbiter.

4190. One can be wise and still fail.

4191. Only the wise find wisdom in silence.

4192. The clever give answers, but the wise ask questions.

4193. The least wisdom is found in those who think themselves wise.

4194. The wise conceive many a thought
with commitment to none,
while the rest are often caught
by a thought they can't outrun.

4195. There is wisdom in expecting the unexpected.

4196. There is wisdom in knowing when silence is your best contribution to a conversation.

4197. There is wisdom in the recognition that the failure to achieve some goals is success.

4198. Thoughts flow on life's flood of tears.

4199. We are more likely to be wise in public than in private matters.

4200. We touch upon wisdom when we see its unattainability.

4201. Wisdom comes when we discover we are wrong.

4202. Wisdom conceals what folly reveals.

4203. Wisdom is doing right without the threat of might.

4204. Wisdom is driven by second thoughts.

4205. Wisdom is failure's prize.

4206. Wisdom is knowledge of ignorance.

4207. Wisdom is learning sculpted by experience.

4208. Wisdom is sweet serenity,
many are prone to say;
those who approach its lofty heights
pay dearly on the way.

4209. Wisdom is the silence found in knowing we can't know.

4210. Wisdom knows the difference between the valuable and invaluable.

4211. Wisdom knows when it is best not to get what you want.

4212. Wisdom prepares while folly ensnares.

4213. Wisdom recognizes the trivial.

4214. Wisdom sees happiness as benevolent blindness to life's harsh realities.

4215. Wisdom sees mystery in the self-evident.

Wishes

4216. Perhaps it's best to lose the race
when we love what we do.
Granted wishes leave no trace
of passion that we knew.

4217. There is a time we yearned to see
that never came to pass,
a part of our reality
beyond the hourglass,
a wish that lives alas.

4218. Wishing can be the fatal flaw of those who fail to
value what they already have while in pursuit of a
future that may never come.

Wit

4219. Genuine wit seeks truth, not its appearance
through a clever condemnation of conventional
wisdom.

4220. The cleverness we call wit
is disinclined to admit
it never votes to acquit.

4221. To praise our kind is rare indeed;
our wit is prone to blame.
More natural to plant the seed
of villainy and shame
with wisdom in our name.

4222. Wit finds that differences are more apparent than real and that similarities are superficial at best.

4223. Wit is a torment of unfulfillment; novelty is its daily bread.

4224. Wit sees commonalities
that bring truth to light,
sees deeper than credulity
to subtleties of sight
that rarely unite.

4225. Wit is the thought of yours or mine
that soars above the rest,
its timeless truth in the bloodline
of writers at their best.

Women

4226. A woman's beauty is brought into question when she is called bright.

Wonder

4227. Every branch of knowledge ends in wonder.

4228. The purpose of both philosophy and science is to weaken wonder.

4229. The wonders of the world deserve more wonder.

4230. To answer all important questions would be disastrous, for we need to wonder.

4231. To wonder is wonderful
to those immersed in doubt.
To know is regrettable
without a single bout
where point and counterpoint
never call time-out.

4232. When wonder inspires worship, thought is replaced with mindless belief.

4233. Wonder is an admission of ignorance.

Words

4234. A great thought can be buried under an avalanche of words. Speak plainly.

4235. Among the many who use the word *calculus* in everyday speech, I suspect few are familiar with the mathematics.

4236. Our words draw a self-portrait without our permission.

4237. Our words, once spoken, belong to the world. There are many thoughts best kept in the limbo of consciousness.

4238. Our words reveal both truth and lies,
      are often best when they surprise
      with life that springs right from the page
      with feelings found in every age.

4239. Some words are better than action.

4240. Some words wrap round truth with the precision
      of a surgeon's scalpel, whereas others wander
      freely in a world of their own.

4241. The tongue, with subtle treachery, wreaks wounds
      that never heal.

4242. The words we use, particularly in poetry, can lead
      us to new and profound thoughts.

4243. Those who use words creatively are oblivious to
      the constrictive grip of grammar.

4244. Unspoken words can be the kindest of all.

4245. Words can be sent into battle or the bedroom
      with equal efficacy.

4246. Words can outweigh actions when they effectively
      explain.

4247. Words found in short supply
      do not have space to lie.

4248. Words innocently pour forth, never knowing
      what harm they may bring.

4249. Words that provoke feelings override any impulse
      to think.

4250. Words will never go out of fashion, for they create beauty comparable to the splendor of the cosmos.

Work

4251. Good work is rewarded by being allowed to continue.

4252. In all of work, the first person you work for is yourself.

4253. Much work is reduced to routine tasks that offer little incentive to engage the creative impulse.

4254. Those who are saved by work lack imagination.

4255. Emulating ants, with their small steps of continuous application, is the first step to effective work.

4256. To work effectively, one must accept one's imperfections.

4257. "What would I do?" is the cry of all who prefer the demands of the workplace to the burden of freedom.

4258. Work has saved more than one tormented soul from otherwise unendurable tragedy.

4259. What constitutes work is not well-defined. One person's work is another's amusement.

World

4260. Those who say the world is eternally beautiful must lovingly embrace the endless cycles of birth and death.

Worry

4261. Our species has conceived of a savior, which has enjoyed some success in eliminating worry.

4262. Since everything ends badly, don't worry.

4263. Worry is a thoughtful pursuit of catastrophe.

4264. Worry is fine if it gives rise to preparation.

4265. Worry is the curse of an intelligent species who can see beyond the next meal.

Worship

4266. Those who worship expect something more than the pleasure of dropping to their knees in adoration.

4267. Worship of someone far above
is fear that finds its way
to claims of most profound love
that deftly saves the day—
seems heaven's easy prey.

4268. To worship what is kind and good
is a faultless pursuit.
To worship gods and goddesses
is sometimes a route
to cruelty unmatched,
in the name of God to boot.

Worth

4269. An enemy's envy is preferable to a friend's praise.

4270. For many, one's bank account is inversely related to character.

Writing

4271. A world of loving perfection would be a writer's hell.

4272. A writer allows his mind to be an open book.

4273. A writer hopes to be understood, but not too well.

4274. A writer is unlikely to be well-known for subtlety, for the audience is likely to be small.

4275. A writer may return to a theme repeatedly, searching for words that compel us to quote.

4276. Aphorists may express one thought at one moment and an opposing thought the next. Truth may be somewhere in between.

4277. Authors are often willing to reveal in public what they would never say in private.

4278. Books should court truth, not the favor of potential readers.

4279. Can roaring reality ever be caught in the net of language?

4280. Clarity of thought and language can be deceptively profound.

4281. Composition difficult to understand is often easy to write.

4282. Composition worth the space knows when to erase.

4283. Fiction reveals the author in the characters.

4284. For me, the marriage of sense and sound is as important as thought.

4285. For the writer, creativity of thought is problematic. To think beyond Relativity is rare.

4286. For the written word to be compelling, it must speak with the naked voice of the confessional.

4287. Good writing is fueled by passion and subdued by reason.

4288. Great writers can make the familiar live again
with the vitality of a newborn.

4289. Great writers take a common thought
and make all feel they have been taught.
Word magic is the game they play;
thought is reborn on that day.

4290. Great writing cannot survive poor reading.

4291. Great writing is done so well,
words appear to roll off the tongue.
The writer knows the endless throes
found in a sentence soundly strung.

4292. Great writing weaves style and substance into
unforgettable lines of literature.

4293. I am not a professional writer, merely one who
loves the language and the process.

4294. I began writing at seventy, joining those who love
language and thought.

4295. I write to provoke thought, not to induce belief or
make money.

4296. If a writer aspires to write literature, it is unwise
to ask the approval of publishers, critics, or the
public.

4297. If we could escape the tenor of our time, would
anyone listen?

4298. If you do not write for yourself, your words and
thoughts belong to another.

4299. If your lines reverberate
with strains of simple truth,
the music of the written word
has found eternal youth.

4300. In writing and thought, I prefer the
quintessential.

4301. My books speak of what is true
for me—and perhaps for you.

4302. My writings simply do portray
feelings deep and true that say
I lived and loved along the way.

4303. Not every reader is found to be
responsive to subtlety,
so find a way to please the ear
when thoughts reach for a frontier.

4304. Quietly believe your book is great.
Do your best and leave the rest to fate.

4305. Reply to publishers: the only valid credential is
the work itself.

4306. Simple language allows thought to take center
stage.

4307. Sound is as important as sense in good writing.
We write with our ears.

4308. The favor of fools may be profitable but is surely
not rewarding.

4309. The flow of blood is seldom caught by the flow of language. Words stop at life's door.

4310. The self-published are ignored, whereas those published at the expense of another are given serious consideration. Can it be that publishers have artistic acumen as well as a hunger for profit?

4311. The unknown writer can speak the truth with relative impunity.

4312. The writer discovers that writing well is not enough; one must also be able to think.

4313. The writer who makes a common thought memorable has not failed.

4314. The writer who requires perfection will never publish.

4315. The writer's goal is in the end
to wrap a thought in words so fine
that all who read will comprehend
the life we put into each line.

4316. There is originality in form as well as substance. If you say something better than anyone else, it belongs to you.

4317. Those who write fiction can more easily speak their truth; the aphorist has no disguise.

4318. Those who write of humankind will have few readers, but writing of a particular human will excite the appetite for gossip and more.

4319. To create from the turmoil of experience is the writer's task.

4320. To wander through this marvelous world of possibilities, creating sentences of sense and sound that probe every aspect of life, is the joy of writing.

4321. To write for the public is to pursue marketable mediocrity. Those with a passion for writing write for themselves, with the hope that some few will appreciate the effort.

4322. Unknown writers sometimes console themselves with the unlikely prospect of posthumous birth.

4323. Well said is well done.

4324. With foggy thinking, words run out of sight; some see darkness as a shining light.

4325. Writers feed on the foibles of humanity.

4326. Writers of fiction know only one genre.

4327. Writers return to favorite themes, irresistibly drawn to the unresolved.

4328. Writing can bring a depth to thought unknown in direct conversation, for there is no distracting physicality.

4329. Writing is beautiful when it expresses every nuance of meaning in the fewest words.

4330. Writing is building with words. We can judge the edifice of our thoughts by its foundation in truth.

4331. Your writing should reflect your own vision and style and should never be influenced by the critics who abound.

Wrongdoing

4332. Beyond the unforgivable, a test of a civilized society is a second chance.

Yes and No

4333. To reply with yes
to avoid distress
may bring tranquility.
But an honest no
will clearly show
staunch integrity.

Youth

4334. Age is found looking back
on paths that went awry;
youth is seen in a new dream,
compelling us to try.

4335. In youth, death is a remote possibility that grows with the years into a hideous reality, where those we love simply disappear.

4336. Inexperience is the greatest weakness and strength of youth.

4337. It is strange to see the young uncomfortable with the old when most young people wish to live a very long time.

4338. My youth is vague recollection
of triumph and despair;
age is thoughtful speculation
in books I write with care.

4339. The affectations of youth are a desperate attempt to escape the inevitable.

4340. The beauty of youth may, for a time, make tolerable youth's nonsense.

4341. The conformity of youth is clearly seen in their opposition to parental advice.

4342. The conformity of youth makes war possible.

4343. The experience of age
is the folly of youth.
Mistakes make the sage,
the only road to truth.

4344. The faith of youth rarely survives the turmoil of age. The more thoughtful we become, the less we believe.

4345. The thought of return to youth,
with its timely torment,
the missteps and reproof
that invade each moment,
is too much to endure;
youth has lost its allure.

4346. There is intellectual barrenness in a generation
that finds video games more vital than
philosophy.

4347. There is youthful old age in a writer beyond
eighty.

4348. Those who put their faith in youth find no value
in experience.

4349. Youth is a matter of yearnings, not years.

4350. Youth is a template for all that follows.

4351. Youth is experimental and full of mistakes that
should not mark one for life.

4352. Youth prefers to make its own mistakes,
unencumbered by the wisdom of age.

4353. Youth steps out on dancing feet,
feels joy in every move;
age walks in pain with a cane
with nothing more to prove.

4354. Youth strives to become somebody, while age
confronts the inevitable.

4355. Youthful beauty fails to make palatable the inevitable indiscretions of the young.

Zeal

4356. Religious zeal is a desperate attempt to escape the inevitable.

Epilogue

The work is done with some regret,
for there is more to say.
I only hope that it has met
a standard on the way
that time will not betray.

About the Author

Donald Redheffer was born in 1935 and is a graduate of DePaul University. Although he is a retired teacher of mathematics, his first loves are philosophy and poetry. The author of *Musings of a Meandering Stream*, *Streams of Thought*, *Reply to Oblivion*, and *Sense and Sound*, he is also an accomplished nature photographer. Mr. Redheffer spent his formative years in Park Ridge, Illinois. He now resides in Chicago with his wife, Joselita Redheffer.

CPSIA information can be obtained
at www.ICGtesting.com
Printed in the USA
FSOW02n0711091117
40962FS